Essays
On The
Media

by James Rozoff

Table of Contents

NOTE:

The focus of this book is squarely on the media. I do not wish to prove that the media is right or wrong on any given issue so much as point out how the media does not act like they are interested in getting a given story right at all, but instead wish to support the narratives of the wealthy and powerful. You might disagree with many of the issues I seem to defend, and that is fine. You can believe that the media has a particular story right while still admitting the many ways in which they failed in their basic journalistic obligations in reporting on it.

Perhaps the issue more likely to hit a nerve with many is the issue of Russian interference in the U.S. elections. But whatever your thoughts on the Russiagate narrative might be, it would be impossible to discuss the media without discussing it. It has been the dominant story of the last decade. You are welcome to believe any and every aspect of Russian interference the media has reported—from spy whales to pee tapes to Pokemon Go!—but I still encourage you to keep an open mind as to HOW they were reported and whether or not we as a society benefit from a media that repeatedly proves itself unwilling to uphold the minimum standards of journalism. Media literacy among the common citizenry is necessary for a functioning government, and the degree to which it is being taught has dropped sharply in the last few decades.

The Third Parent

Nearly two decades ago, I got it into my head to write a book about the influence of television on our culture. I was torn between the titles "The Third Parent" and "Adulthood's End".

The main premise behind it was that television took over the role of parent in the household. While up until that time parents were the primary role models and authorities in the household, television usurped those roles. And unlike actual parents, television never aged, its position as the maker of decisions never waned.

Most people take on the more difficult aspects of being the adult in the family out of necessity. As parents are no longer able to care for themselves, their children are forced into making decisions for them they had hoped never to have to make. They realize there is no authority who can make the tough decisions for them, that Mom and Dad are no longer their protectors but dependent upon them. This is a rite of passage we all must go through. But as television never ages, we never pass that rite, never assume the mantle of maturity. Television is always going to be the one to tell us how to behave, how to dress, what narratives to believe, which culture to consume. As the television only transmits and never receives, how could the relationship ever be otherwise?

I look back on the first time it started to dawn on me that television was usurping the position of authority in the household. It was the latter part of the 1970s and President Carter was discussing the fuel shortage. He gave a simple suggestion to turn our heat down a few degrees and wear a sweater if we were cold.

It was the sort of advice our parents would have given us, and that was the problem. You see, the first generation of children raised on television were now grown up and we did not want to listen to our parents anymore. We preferred to listen to our televisions because the television always told us what we wanted to hear. The television told us we deserved a break today, that sugary snacks were good for us, women were made to be ogled and there were no repercussions to casual sex.

And so a new politician emerged to tell us of the new and improved classic homemade way of doing things. The television had a lovechild and he was called Ronald Reagan. He would explain our world the way we wanted to hear it, just like all those other neat guys on TV. We wanted a handsome and winning personality, not our stuffy old dad. We wanted Ronald Reagan, not Jimmy Carter. We wanted Hannity, not Colmes.

We could have whatever we wanted. You go, girl, you deserve it. We could have whiter teeth AND fresher breath. We didn't have to live with ring around the collar or waxy yellow buildup anymore. So when the voters went to the polls in November of 1980, the changes that had begun in the 1950s with the widespread infiltration of televisions in homes had finally come to fruition.

In the 60s they spoke of a generation gap. It is curious that this expression was almost uniquely applied to the rift that occurred between the first generation to be raised on television and the last to be raised without it. But once that generation that had been raised on television began to raise another generation that was being raised on television, the term generation gap faded from conversation. The Baby Boomers understood the attitudes their children had, because they had both been raised by The Third Parent. Baby Boomers were determined to be different from their parents. They would never grow up. Not really. They were still children in the eyes of the never-aging television.

The shift had taken place and the rift between generations, the one television had caused, was soon forgotten. Never again would we have to listen to adults. Nor would we ever be expected to become adults ourselves. We were all free now to leave the unpleasantness of making difficult decisions behind us. The only choosing we had to make was whether we would drink Miller Lite or Bud Light. We were the Pepsi generation and we were never going to grow old (or up).

There was a new authority now, although we never chose to really think about it that way. We didn't need parents anymore nor did we have to become them. We could be friends to our children rather than rule-makers or —God forbid— role models. We could use the time we weren't busy making money to spend it. We could buy for a second time all the toys of our youth and never have to be responsible for anything.

Because, after all, authority was not given to us, it belonged to the market place. By merely choosing between Pepsi or Coke, magic forces would make the world into a Heaven for us all. Authority was decreed through television waves that mystically traveled through the air and into the privacy of our houses. Complex decision making was uncool, we wanted our nation's problems to be solved as easily and completely as Jack Tripper's problems were every Tuesday night on ABC.

As for getting older, well, that was something our parents did. We would have none of that, because growing older meant taking on responsibility, and television would take that burden from us. All we had to do was stay up on the latest trends, buy the products that were currently trendy. We just had to listen to the same music our kids did, pretend to find some value in it. Forget about finding meaning in our own lives, we had to find ways to relate to our children, even if in the end all we did was validate the line being sold to them by the advertisers.

When the lines and the droopiness and receding hairlines and erectile dysfunction showed up, television was there with the answers. Our skin could look as smooth as Joan Rivers', our boobs as perky as any saline-bag celebrity. And for guys, hey, it was just like the 60s, only the drugs now were Rogaine and Viagra. Death was only an illusion, which meant we never had to worry too much about figuring what life was all about. All we had to do was hang onto our youth. All we had to do was keep flunking Maturity 101 so we never had to graduate.

Adulthood's End

If you look around you might find a few, there are still some left. But they are fading quickly, the oldest ones descending into a second childhood. They were the ones who told stories with morals to them, without the swear words. They were the ones who told you not to take anything you weren't intending to eat and to eat whatever you took. They lived in the real world and learned their lessons the hard way. Tom Brokaw called them The Greatest Generation, but in truth they were merely the last of the adults.

My dad was six years old when The Great Depression hit. The Great Depression ended for him when the Great War began. And after that, well maybe his generation just got tired of great troubles. They'd paid their dues and deserved a little peace and prosperity. Maybe they wanted to try great consumption instead. Maybe they just wanted to finally live life and get a little enjoyment out of it. There's nothing wrong with that, after all. You can't blame people for wanting to avoid suffering and sacrifice if they can get away with it. And we were a country on the rise, reaching peaks never experienced before.

There's the bitch of it, isn't it? I think we can all relate: we struggle and suffer and finally get to a point where we feel we can relax a little, spend a little...and bam, just when we let loose a bit something smacks us when we least expect it. We can never afford to get too comfortable in this life.

But we did get too comfortable. Not so much the greatest generation themselves, they had learned their lessons too severely to ever forget. But when it came to their children, well they did try to instill the values their parents had instilled into them. But times had changed and it was hard to relate such values to a time of never-before-seen prosperity. Besides, there was this thing called mass media, and it screamed from the center of the television, from billboards, and magazines that we were living in a new era where The American Way was a way of consumerism. Technology was the god that provided for us all, and we would hardly be grateful recipients of her blessings if we did not dutifully give homage. In the process, those gods The Greatest Generation worshipped didn't seem so relevant anymore. We began to turn inwards. Well, not really. Actually we turned towards television, which told us our individual needs were greater than any communal needs. We were the land of the free and freedom meant doing your own thing. Of course, deep down, no man is an island unto himself, so doing your own thing leaves one awfully lonely. And when we get lonely, we get scared. And when we get scared we cry out for our mommy. And since mommy was now at work in order to provide for all of those things television said we needed to own, the generations that followed the Greatest Generation found a surrogate parent: television. Television was always there to provide support, to tell us that we were okay, that we were deserving. In fact, it never told us otherwise. Television never disapproved of anything we did. Because television wanted to support our childish needs and desires. That was TV's role, to keep us children in need of an authority figure. There were many institutions paying millions of dollars to ensure that they had receptive minds in front of them, minds that could shift smoothly from a talking puppet show host to a cartoon shill for sugary cereal.

There's a book called The Hidden Persuaders. It deals with the ways advertisers play to those parts of our psyche that act beneath our conscious mind so that they might appeal to our baser instincts. The book was written in 1957, so Heaven knows how much deeper the propaganda machine is able to burrow into our minds nowadays. But seeing how The Hidden Persuaders was a chilling read in its day, and that the trend has only increased since, it's safe to say the reality of the situation would be jarring and frightening to the average person if the truth were to hit home. So much so that they would most likely be willing to climb back into the hole they've been living in their entire lives. The discrepancy for most people between what they perceive reality to be and what reality truly is, is pretty vast. And while we would all like to think we would be Neo in The Matrix, AKA the chosen one, most of us would rather avert our gaze and continue upon the comfortable path we are walking. That, however, is the same psychological motivation that leads animals to the slaughterhouse.

You're Not A Customer To The Media, You're What's Being Sold

If you don't pay for the news you receive, what you receive is not news, it is propaganda. Propaganda is free, just like slop is free to pigs. It's not given because they appreciate you as a living being, it's given in order to turn you into sausage at some later date. Because, although most people haven't realized this yet, you're not the customer. The customer is always right, but it ain't you.

It's easy to tell who the customer is: the customer pays money. That's why the customer is always right, because businesses are out to make money.

So who pays for the media? An overwhelming amount of media is paid for by advertisers. They are the real customers, they are the ones media has to please in order to get the cheddar. Please the advertisers, make money. Displease them, no money. Get it? You can feed pigs caviar, but it doesn't help the bottom line.

So who are we, we who watch the news? We are the consumers, and that is quite a different thing than customers, although we feel as though we're being catered to, just as the pig comes to believe the farmer owes it to him to dole out the slop on a regular schedule.

And it is slop. You, me, Republican, Democrat, we have no illusions the content we are consuming is high-quality. We know it's not nutritious stuff we're swallowing, but it does kind of taste good going down. In a fatty, salty, processed kind of way.

Do you know why Facebook was telling its users "always free, always will be" a few years back? Because they know if they started charging, you'd leave. Or at the very least, you'd start demanding Facebook cater to your needs. That's the last thing Facebook wants because they're already making billions. Mark Zuckerberg is worth somewhere in the range of $172 billion. How much is that compared to the ordinary Facebook user's net worth? A lot. A whole fucking lot. More a lot than your puny mind can comprehend. Way more a lot than Mark Zuckerberg's mind can comprehend, and he's spent a lot of time contemplating it.

Now you may ask, how did Mark Zuckerberg get so incomprehensibly rich giving you Facebook for free? What, have you already forgotten what I said about the pig and the slop?

That's right, you're not only the consumer of slop, you are the product Mark Zuckerberg sells. You're the pork chops. He sells your information to those who profit from your information. If you've stopped believing the Tooth Fairy pays you money for your teeth, you can stop believing that Facebook gives you something for nothing.

All the media is in the hands of obscenely rich people who are not interested in making you one iota smarter. In fact, they work really hard to keep you stupid. Looking around, I have to say I'm impressed by their success. Although $172 billion is a hell of an incentive.

Your stupidity keeps the advertisers and the media really wealthy. Why would you think they are on your side? Why would you believe the sales pitch they are selling? They want you to eat Doritos and drink Mountain Dew, for fuck's sake.

As wealthy as Zuckerberg is, that's still nothing compared to the net worth of Jeff Bezos, who currently is worth a shit-ton and some change. I say shit-ton and some change because none of us could ever really get our heads around how much fucking money he really has. Jeff Bezos can't figure it out either, all he knows is it isn't enough. Amazon and Whole Foods and the Post Office aren't enough for him, he has to buy a newspaper, too. That'll add a few bucks to his pile. Something comparable to a brick in the Great Wall of China, though, so you gotta wonder why he'd waste his time buying the Washington Post. Maybe, just maybe, because the readers aren't really customers, they're just consumers. He's not making his money selling papers, he's making his money by making you believe he's only there to give you what you've come to expect to see in your trough.

The life of a pig isn't so bad, I guess. It must be pretty okay, because I've never ever heard of a pig uprising, although maybe that's just because the media has never saw fit to tell us about it. More likely, however, the pigs have come to think that they are the customer, that they are the ones being catered to. But should they ever discover the truth...

People Still Read (If The Writer's Worth Reading)

Writers (columnists, journalists, pundits, essayists, etc.) nowadays are not paid to get people to think, they are paid to tell people what to think. They are not even there to be read, their entire word count is just there as window dressing for a headline. The idea is, you see the headline, dive into the first paragraph, become bored, and trust that the rest of the article actually backs up what the headline asserts. Honestly, most people don't even make it to the first paragraph, they just read the headline to learn what people in their group are supposed to be supporting, and take their marching orders. If tomorrow a headline read that a given country was doing something bad to another country, they would put the appropriate flag emoji in their bios. If the headline said another letter or symbol was added to LGBTQ+, they would throw their support 100% behind it without ever bothering too much about what it was. We live in a world where instructions are given through headlines.

If someone like Paul Krugman or Max Boot wrote an opinion piece for the NYT and put "blah blah blah" in every paragraph save the first, 90% of NYT subscribers would never notice. All that would matter is that some well-paid and fêted columnist was saying how good a job Joe Biden was doing. Message received and imprinted. The reader knows the paper is a trusted source, assumes it only hires the best and the brightest, and figures they know what they're talking about. I mean, for Christ sake, Paul Krugman won a Nobel Prize in Economic Science! When he suggests Democrats just saved civilization, who are you to question?

If people took the time to read Krugman or Boot — critically — they would realize how completely they serve the powerful and how invested they are in convincing people that we are living in the best of all possible worlds so long as neoconservatives or neoliberals are permitted to enact their agenda. By extension, if people were to critically read their writing, they would realize how completely it is the job of their publishers to uphold the status quo, a status quo in which the rich are continually getting richer, freedom of speech is being restricted, the environment is circling the drain, and the hands of the Doomsday Clock are as close to midnight as they've ever been.

Because people don't even read the writers they take their cues from, it gives them perfect justification for not reading the writers they disagree with (or more appropriately, the writers they are told they are supposed to disagree with). Chris Hedges had a show on RT? Why would I waste my time on him? Caitlin Johnstone doesn't work for the Washington Post? Then she is not worth my valuable time (which I will use to binge-watch all 8 seasons of some show over a weekend). And didn't I read somewhere that Glenn Greenwald was a fascist? Bit by bit, the number of journalists and commentators is whittled down to a few approved elites. Which very few of you will read, far less of you will share, and even less of you will be able to draw your own thoughts from and connections to.

In their defense, many of these esteemed journalists, pundits and opinion shapers have their work hidden behind a paywall, so it is not always possible to share their work. But this works in their favor because their work is not intended to be read, just their headlines. Hiding their work behind a paywall is the best of both worlds because their headlines are still able to do their work while the risk of someone actually reading their work is lessened.

It is said people don't read anymore, that there is too much information being thrown their way for them to have the time and attention span to immerse themselves in a 2,000 word essay. This is not so. True, people's desire to read is diminished by so much of the writing that is pushed down our throats and is not intended to be read, work meant to confuse rather than enlighten. But people still read. I do so every day. People who don't would like to believe somehow that nobody else has the time or the inclination to do so either, and become defensive and hostile to people who do. "Christ, man, I've read fourteen different headlines today alone, what more could you possibly tell me?"

In a way it is a golden age of political writing. While lacking the backing of large organizations with the means to deploy journalists across the world or defend them from powerful interests, people like Caitlin Johnstone, Glenn Greenwald, and Chris Hedges are writing truly courageous articles. Black Agenda Report and FAIR (Fairness And Accuracy In Reporting) should definitely be on your radar. Sensing that these are desperate times, writers are not holding back. And readers, thirsty for honest and fearless writing, are responding. I see it every day, the passion with which people share the articles of their favorite writers.

The truth is, people will read if you give them something worth reading. The establishment intelligentsia are not worthy of being read, and they're training people to believe that even the (presumed) best writers are not very interesting. Their writing does not connect with the average person because the writers hired by corporate papers and magazines know little or nothing about average people. They speak to those in their group who inhabit the same bubble, those of the PMC (Professional Managerial Class). They are there to tell us what to think, because presumably we would not be able to think without them.

I am encouraged because people actually read what I write. People actually comment on what I write, and share my writing with others. Often they will highlight salient points of my articles, which lets me know they actually paid attention. In this age where writing seems *passé*, I am still able to connect with my fellow human beings through often involved pieces of prose.

I may not have a huge following, but I have managed to acquire a few fans. And I see my work and the work of others like me shared on social media more than I see the work of writers from the big newspapers and magazines being shared. Assuredly it is because my feed is biased and the work of the professionals is often reserved for paying customers, but I also think it's true that people really aren't interested in what they say or how they say it.

Go ahead, tell me the last columnist you read (besides me, of course). Share with me some insight imparted to you, tell me how it made you want to tell others about it. And if you're having trouble calling to mind what it might be, if you yourself have to admit you're not inclined to read a semi-involved bit of writing on what is happening in the world today, perhaps it is not your fault. Check out some of the names I've mentioned and perhaps you will find writing worthy of your time, your attention, your admiration. Perhaps you will be reminded — or shown for the first time — what power can be found in the written word.

Who Can We Trust Regarding Julian Assange?

(Originally published on Medium on June 22, 2022)

The argument is that Julian Assange revealed truths that put American lives at risk. To date, I am unaware of any casualties resulting from Wikileaks' revelations, but let's for a moment assume this argument has merit. If it is just and lawful to imprison a foreign journalist for costing American lives by revealing the truth, isn't it worse still for Americans to tell lies that lead to American deaths? And since the United States was lied into a war in Iraq, a war that has so far cost the lives of nearly 7,000 Americans, shouldn't the people who participated in the lie spend the rest of their lives in prison, as Julian Assange is destined to do?

This would include the entire U.S. media and the entire political class. Let's throw Tony Blair into gaol as well, because he is every bit as much to blame for lying us into Iraq. So what if he's not a U.S. citizen, neither is Julian Assange. This would seem to be the logical first step if one were concerned about setting a precedent that would save American lives. Wouldn't it?

Nearly 7,000 lives lost due to the lies told about Iraq's alleged weapons of mass destruction. Add to that 30,000 wounded. Add to that 1 in 5 soldiers who served in Iraq ending up with PTSD. I'm not good with numbers, but that seems way worse than the hypothetical damage caused by any secrets Julian Assange revealed. In fact, I've never heard anything as bad as a stubbed toe that anyone could blame Assange for.

If we are willing to say non-American lives also have some degree of worth, the amount of deaths resulting from the lies of our media and politicians regarding Iraq approaches a million, according to some estimates. Let me remind you that these are not theoretical deaths that could conceivably result from the lies of our thought leaders, these are real blown apart and decomposing corpses we're talking about.

But somehow the lies that caused so much death to U.S. soldiers aren't worth punishing, while the non-existent casualties and theoretical damage caused by Julian Assange's truth must be dealt with in the harshest of terms, lest others be tempted to follow in Assange's truth-telling footsteps and potentially place American lives in theoretical jeopardy.

I'm starting to believe it's not American lives that those who wish to imprison Assange care about. The more I think about it, the more I realize that all those politicians and media figures who told all the lies and cost so many Americans (and others) their lives are the same ones who are so concerned that Assange must be taught a lesson. Go ahead, Google what the architects of the Iraq War think about Assange. George W. Bush cancelled a speaking engagement when he learned Assange would be speaking at the same event. Bill Krystol had this to say about Assange and Wikileaks: "Why can't we use our various assets to harass, snatch or neutralize Julian Assange and his collaborators, wherever they are? Why can't we disrupt and destroy WikiLeaks in both cyberspace and physical space…? Why can't we warn others of repercussions from assisting this criminal enterprise hostile to the United States?" On and on, the same people who are concerned with the truth that *may* cause harm to befall Americans are those who employed lies to cause immense harm to befall Americans (and others) in real life.

Boy, I wonder who's telling the truth here? The numbers and the clout seem to belong to those who told and continue to tell lies that result in immense suffering and death not only to Americans but to millions of people around the world. I mean, the entire media and political elite couldn't possibly be lying about the danger posed by the truths revealed by Julian Assange, could it?

The Gross Distortions In Russian Media

Sadly, the Russian people are hopelessly lied to by their media. So much so that many Russian people are not even aware of how propagandized they really are. When the media is so omnipresent, when a single narrative is repeated so incessantly and for so long, it is hard for people to realize they are living in an artificially constructed consciousness bubble. People so utterly misinformed are easily manipulated.

Russian media will never show the Russian people the corpses of children blown up by Russian artillery. Not only that, Russian media has spent the last eight years propagandizing the Russian people by showing only the corpses of children in the Donbas region of Ukraine who were killed by the Ukrainian government and the paramilitary groups they allow to function. They fill the eyes of their audience only with images of the bodies burned to death by pro-government factions in Odessa following the U.S.-backed coup in Ukraine. They fill their audience's ears only with the audio of U.S. deep state agent Victoria Nuland openly discussing who they will select as the next president of Ukraine. And they fill their minds only with the fear of the advanced missile systems NATO is placing on the borders of their country.

Russia media shows Ukrainian neo-Nazis openly discussing their violent ideologies and saying how killing people is fun, while sneering at Western values and mocking homosexuals. Meanwhile, they ignore the problems Russia has with homophobia and nationalism.

Russian media does not show their people the acts of violence perpetrated by Russian soldiers. Instead, it shows images and videos of people being tied to lamp posts and beaten by Ukrainians. They show how Roma and other non-Ukrainian people have their faces painted green and their pants removed as they are wrapped to telephone poles with cellophane.

Russian media does not show the brutality Russian soldiers engage in against surrendered Ukrainian soldiers. Why would they? It does not suit their propaganda purposes. Instead, it shows Ukrainians shooting captured Russian soldiers in the leg, then beating them as they bleed to death.

Russian media does not show how Ukrainian prisoners are being used as propaganda pawns by Russia. It only shows how Ukrainian soldiers send images of the corpses of Russian soldiers to the soldiers' families in Russia.

Russian media does not show the cheering mobs greeting the Ukrainian military, it only shows the people greeting the Russians as liberators. It never interviews Ukrainians saying how angry they are to have been overrun by the Russian army, it only talks to those who say how glad they are to have been liberated.

The Russian media have no interest in telling their people how they are killing Ukrainians. Instead, they tell them about how many people have died in Afghanistan and how many Afghani people are still dying because of U.S. sanctions. They don't mention how Russian arms manufacturers are profiting from war, instead they tell their people about how the U.S. is selling weapons to Saudi Arabia that are being used in a war that has killed hundreds of thousands of men, women, and children in Yemen. Instead of showing the bombs exploding in Ukraine, it shows the bombardment of Gaza by Israel and asks why the U.S. never condemns this sort of action from their ally.

Turn on Russian media and you will see the ruins of cities in Libya, Iraq and Syria. For some reason, they're more than willing to discuss the egregious crimes of the United States, while on the crimes of their own government they remain silent. They show pictures of hooded and stripped Iraqi prisoners being abused by U.S. soldiers while ignoring the beam that is in the eye of Russia.

In the four years when the U.S. media was breaking story after story about Russia's involvement in electing Donald Trump, Russian media never once probed deeply into the allegations of a pee tape video and instead only mentioned it when referring to some of the less-substantiated allegations such as Russia using spy dolphins, spy beluga whales, and Pokemon Go!.

It is hard to blame the Russian people themselves. They are, after all, subjected to a degree of sophisticated propaganda unimagined by people of previous generations. It is hard for people who have not only not been given the proper facts but also have been deluged with an erroneous worldview to have a nuanced and well-rounded view of world events. Nevertheless, it is hoped that the lies they are fed become so odious, the narrative they are told to believe so absurd, that they might awaken from their dreamworld and see things as they truly are.

Here's hoping that the people of Russia demand more of their media, so that in the future they might have access to the kind of quality programming and in-depth reporting we now enjoy in the United States.

The Media Makes Me Physically Ill

(Originally published April 23, 2022 on Medium)

I was in high school in the '80s. Back then, you could hear criticism of the media even in the media. Don Henley's Dirty Laundry was on the radio and Albert Brooks' Broadcast News was in the theater. Everybody knew how superficial and unreliable the news we received was…and yet, we somehow ended up believing what it told us.

In the 90s, I had someone knock on the door of my apartment and try to get me to subscribe to cable television. I told him it didn't interest me and it would in no way enrich my life. He tried to tell me that it wasn't all mindless fluff like MTV, that there was The History Channel and A&E. I told him I'm sure many drug addicts have some very fine qualities, but I wouldn't invite them into my home, and I sure wouldn't pay for the privilege of doing so. Yeah, I actually came up with that on the fly and I still remember it 30 years later. Thirty years later, the drug addict he wanted me to pay to have in my home has only gotten worse, as can be witnessed by The History Channel and A&E.

For decades now I have been viewing the mainstream media (MSM) less as a way of informing myself and more as a way of seeing how people were being misinformed. When people would open their mouths and let the media messaging come out, I would be prepared to poke holes in their arguments because I had already heard them.

But the grossness that is the mainstream media has become so bad in the last five years I become physically repulsed by it. In the last month, for the sake of my physical as well as my mental health, I have chosen to avoid it altogether.

You might assume that makes me eminently uninformed, but I assure you there are many other and better ways of receiving information than from corporate media. I still have access to every bit of audio and video I can receive from the television and more, it just doesn't come with a narrative. Well, granted, everyone who relates a story cannot help but put a degree of spin to it, but it is not that overwhelming steamroller narrative I receive when I turn on the TV. Nor is it the condescending opinions of overpaid columnists from the New York Times that have been on the wrong side of every issue for decades. But it will have to do.

I have quit corporate media because I've decided a one-sided conversation with a schizophrenic, pathological liar is not a healthy relationship to be in. I have quit it as one who has long known that he was in a cult and finally found the courage to leave it.

One only needs to have retained some small degree of what they were taught — or should have been taught — in school about how to create a strong argument to see all of the glaring problems with the narratives spun by the millionaire talking heads on the television. You can't assert something in the first paragraph only to contradict it in the second. An 8th grader should know enough to present a balanced argument in order to make a point more forceful. If you leave out known facts because they contradict the argument you are making, you lose credibility. And for the love of God, you have to cite your sources, you can't just write "according to anonymous agents".

The media was obviously bad when I was young. But I never felt personally threatened by it until after 9/11 when the cult of war sprang up in the media. It was around that time that anti-war voices started to be expelled from mainstream media, people like Chris Hedges, Phil Donahue, and Jesse Ventura. It was then that I first fully felt the danger that went along with having opinions differing from the herd. People I worked with echoed the FOX News talking point that anyone opposing war was themselves a threat to the country and should be dealt with accordingly.

Exiled from the mainstream, Hedges, Donahue, Ventura, and many others could be heard for years on RT (referred to in the MSM as a Russian propaganda platform). But their voices have now been silenced there as well, since RT (formerly Russia Today) has been banned from most every platform it was once on.

FOX News was once the channel that demanded patriotism of their viewers, the other news outlets merely demanding it of their staff. Today, however, FOX seems to be the only outlet allowing any kind of dissent at all, and that only from a single personality. As for the rest, those outlets we could once delude ourselves into believing were less pro-war, they have taken the lead. MSNBC's Ali Velshi is calling for direct intervention of NATO with Russia. When did news reporters' job become not reporting the news but actively blowing the bugle for war?

I don't know what the media is like to those living in Russia right now, but I pray it is better than the news we receive here. If that is not the case, I pray the Russian people are better able to see past the warmongering their media is involved in. My hope, my one hope, is that the people are able to see the media the world over for what it is, not a tool for distributing the information people need to help them conduct their own affairs, but as a weapon for those who profit off of war and for those who seek dominance not merely over other nations but over their own people, as well.

Has The American Story Jumped The Shark?

Once upon a time, we all gathered around to watch the American Story play out on TV. It was THE show to watch. It was a simpler time back then, with fewer channels to choose from. And while many of our televisions were unable to show color, still, it was wholesome broadcasting where nobody spoke too cruelly or acted too violently. Good guys were good because they did good things and bad guys were bad because they were mean. Donald Trump would have been a bad guy back then.

Families from the Cleavers to the Bunkers only needed one bread-winner to support the family. Sure, there was a division of expectations among the sexes, but a family only needed one bread winner! Heck, it wasn't even that sexist. Irene Lorenzo was Archie Bunker's next-door neighbor and she was the bread winner, allowing her husband to stay at home. Because the expectation was you didn't need two people working to support a family. And the conservative Archie Bunker never laughed at the idea of an uneducated laborer earning a living wage because HE WAS an uneducated laborer earning a living wage as a forklift operator.

Sometimes the America Show was awful but sometimes it was miraculous. We were so disgusted with such plot twists as the assassinations of Martin Luther King and Robert Kennedy that many of us vowed to stop watching, only to be sucked back in by the amazing sight of a man setting foot upon the moon. As hard as it was to watch sometimes, it was seldom tawdry and often epic. The narrative, as I first came to know it in the early 70s, was that of a flawed character with a troubled past who showed a desire for redemption and was making many of the right moves to atone for past misdeeds.

But I can't help feeling the series has jumped the shark in the last couple of years. Big time. I mean, look at who they have as the leading characters these days, utterly laughable in a not funny sort of way. There's not a one of them who has any depth of character or any real likability factor. How many of them would you want to have to work with or live next to? The Kardashians? Please. The Clintons? I wouldn't trust them around my daughter or my wallet. The Trumps? They're just a retread of The Beverly Hillbillies, what The Flintstones were to The Honeymooners. Plus they're a lot less likable. Hell, I'd take Grannie over Donald any day. And as for the rest, well, there's no contest. At least Jed had some downhome wisdom to him.

And the same plotlines are constantly being rehashed, in Libya as it was in Iraq, in Syria as it was in Libya, with the same situation on the horizon in Iran. "Evil regime oppresses its own people and America must go make everything right." God that one's gotten old. They don't even bother to set up the scene any longer, they just jump right into the violence. No real explanation for it, no build-up with credible characters holding vials full of anthrax, just gratuitous violence. It is spectacle over substance, and it just smacks of desperation. No different from professional wrestling or sleazy daytime soap operas, yesterday's trusted friend becomes today's villain, becomes an ally again tomorrow.

And, oh God, please let them come up with some new villains. Sure, Russia was an intriguing antagonist in the 80s, when you had Sylvester Stallone battling Ivan Drago and fighting in Afghanistan as Rambo, but it hasn't stood the test of time very well. And Russia is not the same (alleged) existential threat as it once was. The storyline has lost all its snap.

It's not just Russia, It's Russia Russia Russia. And the plotline is all over the place. One day the Russians are hacking the French election and the Vermont power grid and the next day that's not a thing. Don't they have anyone working in continuity?

The resolution to every episode is a Deus Ex Machina rather than flowing logically from what we the audience have come to understand. The free market comes down from a cloud to rescue us, or a new hi-tech weapon magically zaps the bad guy or a new miracle drug solves our most pressing problems. In the end, the only solution to any problem is to privatize it, medicate it, or bomb it.

In fact, the entire writing staff seems like they're just going through the paces. They're working for a paycheck rather than having a passion for what the show has meant to so many of us viewers for so long. They're shoveling slop in a trough for us and they're getting paid outrageous sums of money to do it. They seem to have very little connection to the history of the show and the characters and ideas that we came to know and love. Rather than do a little research or grapple with how they can make new events fit in with the history of the show, they simply retcon things or not even bother to reconcile what is happening now to what has gone before.

And all of the main characters, the ones we loved, the ones we were willing to tune in for week after week because they exhibited so many fine and noble and endearing qualities, have been killed off pointlessly in order to make a simplistic and ugly narrative work. And those who haven't been killed have either been marginalized or written out altogether as if they never existed, people like Ralph Nader and Chris Hedges. Sure, they weren't the flashy characters you see nowadays, but they added depth and emotional resonance to the drama. They took a little while to understand, but you loved them the all the more the more you got to know them.

Let's face it, the writers of the script have lost touch with what made the original story so compelling in the first place. They've lost respect for the viewers, the ones who really matter. Instead, they work for the advertisers, slipping in product placement and selling every sort of merchandise they can imagine with the show's logo on it.

We've seen it happen to many of our favorite shows before, and we know that when it gets to this point it won't be long before the show gets cancelled, and fittingly so. It's best we remember it for what it was in its prime rather than allow poor production to tarnish our memories.

This is not to say that there is no way of retrieving it from imminent cancellation. This series can still be saved. In fact it can be made better than it ever was. But to do that, we've got to bring in new script writers, people who are knowledgeable about and reverent of what the show is all about at its core. They're out there. So many dedicated fans of The America Show have been writing their own fan fiction on fan-sites where true aficionados of the show meet and discuss what made it great and what could make it great again. Their work is done not for money but for love. These types of writers would quickly write out the ridiculous cast of characters now dominating center stage, these clowns and floozies who parade in front of the camera oblivious to how sleazy they really are. We've got to bring in compelling actors with integrity, intelligence and character. They're out there, we've got a stack of spec scripts awaiting implementation. We've got a ton of actors' resumes of fresh new faces willing to do daring and edgy work, willing to break new dramatic ground. We're sick of the thin facades and the painted masks that attempt to provide entertainment for us. It is a play designed for children, a ruse meant to dull our senses rather than give us something of substance.

Give us back the story we knew and loved.

The Voices Of Individuals Are Being Silenced, The Voice Of The Machine Reigns Supreme

I woke up this morning thinking I must write like the world depended on it. Because it does.

I truly believe the pen is mightier than the sword, that thoughtful words intent on peace can end wars.

The war machine knows this too, which is why it has its claws deeply embedded into corporate media. Never will you hear the words of peace uttered in the media, seldom if ever will you hear the names of Mahatma Gandhi, Martin Luther King, or Jesus Christ mentioned. What voices for peace that once existed in corporate media have long since been banished. The corporate press has so lost itself in its role of cheerleader for war that the only time they now question government spokespersons is to ask why the United States is not instituting a no-fly zone in Ukraine, a measure likely to open the floodgates to nuclear Armageddon.

I write like the world depends on it, because all nuance and perspective have been stripped from the official narrative. To dare to provide context, to point out just how completely the corporate media are failing at their jobs, is to invite the label of Putin puppet.

I tell myself to write like the world depended on it because otherwise the urge to keep quiet and go along would overwhelm me. Because the power of group-think is immense and I do not wish to cause undue trouble or concern to friends and loved ones. I want my life to be a normal one, filled with the simple pleasures life provides. I've never been the type to draw attention to myself. I like to think I am not one who is addicted to drama, does not like to cause scenes, or make enemies. Believe me when I tell you I have other things I would rather be doing if I did not feel the world depended on me not being silent. There are many books by great thinkers and storytellers that I have not yet opened.

The desire to keep quiet is great. The more the official narrative attains unanimity, the harder it is to speak of anything that is not officially sanctioned, to speak any thought that is my own and not merely repeated from the media. The urge to not simply silence my voice but silence my inner voice as well is hard to resist. To bow to the supposed greater knowledge and wisdom of those in places of power would be such an easing of that weight that is on my mind. It is greatly to be wished.

But when I turn on the media, I realize how impossible that is for me to do. To spend thirty seconds watching any mainstream media outlet is to do damage to my mind, my emotional state of wellbeing, my soul, and my artistic sensibility. Their sense of proportionality is utterly lacking, so that the speck in another's eye is amplified while the moat in their own is ignored. Their desire to dig deeper into issues is absent, their grasp of the subject matter does not extend beyond talking points, their lack of concern for the lives that are ruined by what they are pushing lacks humanity, their inability to speak to spiritual matters betrays their soullessness.

I had this feeling decades ago when I watched the FOX News channel, but now it has spread everywhere. Where once conservative Sean Hannity was forced to argue with liberal Alan Colmes, now there is no challenge to his pronouncements. And so it goes across the spectrum, each personality speaking to an audience that is not challenged to think, each personality in their own way spouting the official narrative with a local vernacular that appeals to their particular audience.

The voices of the talking heads speak not merely with authority but with a demand for compliance. To doubt the media nowadays is to doubt the pronouncements of the church in centuries past. To doubt the information coming from anonymous sources within intelligence agencies is to doubt the proclamations of the king. The term excommunicated has been replaced with the term canceled, but the effects of such an edict can still ruin careers and end in censorship.

I feel the call for uniformity more strongly now than I ever have in my entire life. During the time of 9/11 and the Iraq War, there was still a feeling of party differences, where one could oppose the actions of an administration and still feel part of the political party not in charge. But now the calls for conformity are coming from within the party I once considered my own, and they are not simply calls but shrieks.

I write like the world depends on it, not because I hold any particular insight or knowledge that the world needs to hear but because I know the voice of the individual and the outsider still needs to be heard. The lies and even the truths of those not anointed by the establishment press and the establishment political parties are being silenced, while the lies of the establishment are amplified even when incontrovertible evidence to the contrary is easily obtained.

I write like the world depends on it, because I believe each of us speaking from the truth that is inside of us will shape the world towards beauty and truth far more than us conforming ourselves to work within a machine that seeks to steamroll all unapproved and dissenting voices.

I write like the world depends on it, not because I believe there is greatness in what I say, but from my belief that people communicating openly and without coercion can together achieve greatness.

The narrative by which we all now live our lives is one that is being written not by people motivated by their own inner ideas, but by those willing to serve the machine. And while the machine rewards those who provide value to it, the machine has an agenda of its own. It will squash everything in its path that does not provide it value.

Every living thing on this planet is now in its path.

I write like the world depends on it because my voice is a human voice. For all its flaws and shortcomings it is a voice of an individual in a world filled with the sound of machinery and conformity. Too many of us only see our value in terms of how we can serve the machine, too few of us willing to ask if the machine serves humanity or the long-term viability of life on Earth.

The Media In The Age Of Muhammad Ali

I watched a couple of documentaries on Muhammad Ali recently and was impressed by the interviews they contained. It's only natural to be impressed by the likes of Malcom X and Martin Luther King Jr, both of whom had something to say on Muhammad Ali and the issues that swirled about him. I of course was impressed by Muhammad Ali, as well, who was never afraid to speak his mind. But my respect went far further than that to the opponents of and even the investors in Ali.

Prior to watching Ken Burns' documentary on Ali, I was unaware of how much Ali sided with Elijah Muhammad over Malcom X. Nevertheless, Malcom X always spoke measuredly when talking about Ali, revealing a nuanced approach. Although he was personally involved, he didn't appear to let his own concerns outweigh his overall assessment of the situation. He understood that Ali stood for a lot of issues, many of which were more important than Malcom's disagreements with his former mentor.

Ali, of course, spoke with unreserved openness on most occasions. But he still realized the power of his words to harm, and so on important topics he measured his words and showed respect to even those who opposed him.

It was interesting too to hear from Ali's opponents. Many of them had legitimate disagreements with his actions and his words, both on personal and philosophical matters. They did not hold back on what they felt Ali did wrong in showing disrespect to their own persons or to causes or positions they held dear. Yet there was invariably a respect for Ali, not only for his ability and determination, but also for the strength with which he held his convictions. An opponent, even an enemy, is capable of having respect for someone who demonstrates conviction, heart, and a capacity for self-sacrifice for his principles.

There was also an interview of one of Ali's early investors which I found admirable. They were a group of Kentucky businessmen who thought Ali had talent enough to risk their money on. Yes, they sought to make a profit off him, but I can't help feeling they were investing in Ali not merely because of what they might stand to gain but because they found him as a human being to be someone worthy of their investment. When asked if it embarrassed Kentucky businessmen, who were after all Kentucky Christians, to have a Muslim mouthpiece, one of them replied: "I don't think it's been that embarrassing. Actually, it's been startling. But, in the first place, most of us feel that a man has a right to choose his own religion, his own faith. In the second place, and I have repeated this many times, if the Black Muslims mean hatred, then Cassius (Ali) will never be a true Black Muslim, because he has no hatred for anybody in his soul or in his mind."

What stood out to me was the fact that every one of them spoke from an honest, thoughtful position. It is not all that hard to recognize when someone is speaking from the heart, easier still to recognize when a position is an honestly held one and not mindlessly parroted. Compare that to anything you might come across in the media today. Not more than one in a thousand people you see on TV talks from the heart but instead sticks to the script given him. Whether it be coaches or players talking about a game, politicians talking about their politics, or artists talking about their art, it's hard to find someone who is not simply saying what he has been told to say. The art of public relations has destroyed the ability of the individual to speak the truth within him. And if one should do so, the media itself would do what it could to crush him, as if it cannot permit an honest opinion to reach the masses. Authenticity would be too jarring a contrast to what is presented in the media.

It seems that people in a less media-savvy generation were more prone to speak their own truth. Not only that, being less dominated by media opinions, they worked harder to develop opinions of their own. People were more used to speaking AS individuals TO individuals. Words were more measured and yet also more sincere. Because the words they used were spoken from the truth of a human being, not molded by a machine that tells us what to think and what to say.

I cannot help thinking the media that exists today exists to crush the individual. Perhaps it is only a necessary byproduct of the crushing of the individual, but it tends to crush the ability to think clearly, as well. Assuredly it crushes the tendency to talk respectfully towards others.

I will not go as far as to say the athletes and people in general today are less thoughtful and less genuine than those in the 60s. But I will say the media does all it can to dampen communication between individuals, pushing instead establishment narratives that neither hold up to intelligent scrutiny nor help in any way to make the average person feel more connected to his community and the world. It is my hope that people will come to insist on speaking more from the core of who they are than allowing themselves to conform to the talking points thrust upon them by anonymous authority. And it is my hope also that people will seek alternatives to a media whose job it appears to be to squash legitimate communication in favor of preaching from the establishment pulpit.

The Oligarchy's Attack On Assange Is A Battle Of State Secrecy Against Individual Liberty

It'd be a tough call, but if I had the choice between being tortured to death the way journalist Jamal Khashoggi was and the way Julian Assange is currently being tortured, I'd say "bring on the knives." It would be painful, for sure, but it would be a much briefer form of torture, the yank-the-Band-Aid-off-quickly way to go.

There is a certain cold cruelty to be found in the modern approach that is even more terrifying than the hot savagery of Saudi theocracy. Power held in the hands of a cruel few still offers the possibility for human virtues such as mercy or compassion to be at play, whereas power invested in bureaucracy permits every member of the system to believe they have no obligation to their own morals but only to the higher power of the institution itself. The Western world has, for the greater part, distanced itself from the horrors of the older forms of authority. But it is rushing headlong into a new and potentially more terrifying one.

The very thrust of modern civilization has been towards increasing the rights of individuals while limiting the powers of governments. And I'm being liberal with the word "modern", because it reaches back to the time of the Magna Carta in 1215. It reaches back even to the time of Hammurabi, whose code was written in c. 1792 B.C. and which sought to codify laws to which even the powerful must adhere.

After the Magna Carta, The United States Constitution was the next major milestone in advancing the rights of the individual (well, some individuals) while limiting the power and the right to secrecy of the government. It was a noble piece of paper for its time, one which we have for centuries used to advance the rights of the people to be in charge of their government. I don't recall anything in the U.S. Constitution about the rights of intelligence agencies to privacy.

Our intelligence agencies say they fear that Julian Assange's leaks are putting agents at risk. I rather think that they are trying to silence him, torture him, and possibly kill him not because of the risk he puts particular agents at but because they don't want people knowing about the crimes in which the CIA is involved.

But let us take them at their own word for the sake of argument, and for that sake alone. Never should we trust people with such power and such a degree of secrecy at their word for any other reason but for the sake of argument. Never for any other reason should we trust an agency whose former director admitted "...we lied, we cheated we stole... like, we had entire training courses." If we must choose, it is far better to trust Assange based on his record than the CIA. But for the sake of argument, let us suppose Julian Assange put the lives of CIA operatives at risk.

Good. Because people who are responsible for drone bombing innocent civilians should not be able to do so in anonymity. People who murder from half a world away should not feel safe from reprisal. People who torture should not feel they can do so with utter impunity. No one should be above the law, yet that is precisely what those who work in secrecy are.

It is not that our intelligence agencies occasionally do bad things, it is that they *primarily* do bad things. If they did the occasional good thing, word would leak out. But the post-world-war history is the history of the CIA and its British equivalent doing bad things, written in blood across the globe, in any place former colonies of the West tried to seize sovereignty. They epitomize the opposite of everything the advancement of liberal democracy was working towards. They are an anti-revolutionary force. They are THE anti-revolutionary force. They aim to bring us back to the era a hundred years ago where oligarchic rule was at the peak of its power.

And it is to a hundred-year-old law that they turned to to prosecute Julian Assange. It is the very same Espionage Act they used to prosecute Eugene V. Debs 105 years ago. Eugene Debs, the greatest threat the oligarchy and their two-party system faced at that time. The fact that the average person is unaware of his name or his place in history is evidence that the oligarchs never retreated far from the center of power.

The powerful will employ those who are the experts of law to find rationalizations for their actions, even if they have to go back a hundred years to one of the darkest eras of our country. Legalists will perplex and confound the average citizen with their superior knowledge of the arcane in order to hide the immorality of their actions. The experts will bury in law the obvious wrongness of their behavior.

It is time we move beyond the experts and their manipulations of the law and simply ask, "Is this right? Does this further the cause of individual freedoms in the face of oppressive governments?" We do not all need to become legal scholars, that is neither practical nor possible. Instead, we must strip away the arguments of the legalists and deal with the kind of morality that the common people can wrestle with. That is, if we want a nation ruled by the people — the common people — and not by an elite few who are permitted to work in secrecy and with immunity from the laws by which the rest of us are bound.

If we wish to free ourselves, if we wish to continue our cultural evolution towards greater freedom for the individual and less for oppressive government, we must recognize that our own freedoms are inextricably entwined with Julian Assange's.

Media Played Up Alleged Pee Tape, Ignored Trump's Rape Allegations Tied To Epstein

Soon after Donald Trump was elected president, the news media was alive with innuendo about a possible video of prostitutes peeing on our president elect. No evidence of such a tape existing or such an event ever taking place was given, no direct witnesses stepped forward to collaborate the allegation. It didn't matter. The media ran with it and because of that, everyone heard about it. The source of this rumor was a document paid for by the Democratic Party and the Clinton Campaign.

Fast-forward to last night, when for the first time I heard about the civil lawsuit filed by an anonymous woman who claimed that she had been raped by Jeffrey Epstein AND Donald Trump when she was only 13 years old. Her allegations are corroborated by a second woman, who is also choosing to remain anonymous because she fears retribution.

This is a far more damning allegation than the one the news chose to cover and which people chose to share on social media. And the sources, while choosing to remain anonymous, are more convincing than the Steele Dossier, which years later is being shredded by the very same media that originally chose to uncritically share the most salacious allegations mentioned in it.

Why do you think the media chose to highlight the one while ignoring the other? As embarrassing as the revelation (if true) that Trump paid prostitutes to pee on him, it is merely that, an embarrassing revelation. That is a far cry from accusations of raping a thirteen-year-old. It is very difficult to paint the person peeing on another person as the victim, he who is being peed upon as the victimizer.

Yet the one story is picked up by the media while the other is buried. Strange. "Ah," you say, "but the one involves a foreign government having compromising material on our soon to be president." This is why it is so consequential, even though it is nothing but an utterly unfounded accusation.

But this leads to the question: Just who do you think Jeffrey Epstein is? And if you think that perhaps Epstein was either murdered or was permitted to kill himself, then you must ask yourself: "Who had the influence to get that done?"

Jeffrey Epstein lured people into having sex with minors as a way of blackmailing them. But as Kim Iverson pointed out, a lot of those being blackmailed had more political power than monetary wealth. In other words, Jeffrey Epstein was not interested in money so much as political power. Why? One can only conclude that he was not working for himself but for someone or some ones who were interested in having the goods on powerful people.

Who could that be? I'm not making any accusations, but a foreign government would be a rather obvious guess. A foreign government in close cooperation with our own, judging by the way so many in the media and the criminal justice system looked the other way.

It's not worth my time to speculate on what is the real story behind Jeffrey Epstein. It is far easier to point to those whose job it is to give us the facts behind the matter and say just how poor a job they've done. You can't get a story so wrong for so long without it pointing to a very systemically flawed system.

A system that protects powerful pedophiles is capable of hiding ANY crime, perpetrating ANY atrocity, accepting ANY degree of corruption. It's easy for us to say we are being led by a decadent and corrupt group of elites. It is less easy for us to admit that we've permitted them to get away with it for many years. There needs to be some kind of reckoning, and that will never happen until we are willing to demand more not just of our rulers, but of ourselves as well. However unpleasant this might be, we need to get to the truth on this matter.

The Conspiracy Of Silence Regarding Jeffrey Epstein

You know what MSNBC and FOXNews have in common? Neither one of them has done any sort of investigation into the unlikely suicide of Jeffrey Epstein. Kind of weird, right? I mean, what with his ties to prominent Democrats AND Republicans and all. If you believe the other side is engaged in unhinged conspiracy theories all the time it's kind of shocking that Rachel Maddow and Sean Hannity are ignoring it. I'm guessing it would draw huge ratings. And it's a very suspicious and unlikely official story. At the bare minimum you think they'd be trying to find out who else was involved with Epstein. And yet neither side will touch it.

Why, it almost seems that they're willing to forego sensationalistic journalism that gets huge ratings for some higher interest. And what, pray tell, is of greater interest to corporate media than ratings and the profit they represent?

What we are seeing is a conspiracy of silence. What we are seeing is both sides protecting the powerful who were involved in unspeakable crimes against children.

This isn't in question, is it? I mean, Bill Clinton flew the Lolita Express dozens of times. How is it possible he could be innocent in all of this? And Prince Andrew seems very guilty from all accounts. Do we just let him go because he belongs to a very wealthy and influential family? That doesn't seem to be the sort of thing serious publications like The Washington Post would do. I mean, their motto is "Democracy dies in darkness." Surely they should be shining a little light on an unlikely death that spared powerful people disgrace and prison terms.

How do you explain it? How do you say that the most prominent prisoner on this planet was permitted to kill himself in jail while those who were supposed to prevent that from happening were AWOL and the cameras (plural) that were supposed to be monitoring him both malfunctioned? How is this not a scandal?

It is not a scandal because the mainstream media — all of it, regardless of alleged political bent — did not turn it into one. And they alone have the power to turn a story into a scandal. They can even turn something that's not a scandal into a scandal, like Russiagate, WMDs in Iraq and chemical weapons in Syria. Or the sinking of the Maine. The media is that powerful.

And it is also that unified. At least, in regards to everything that matters to their owners. They may argue mindlessly and endlessly over some issues, but they are issues both sides agree to argue over. They might not be telling you what to think, but they are always telling you what to think about. And what they are not telling you to think about is Jeffrey Epstein and the conspiracy of silence that surrounds him. It is glaringly obvious and unarguable. If you care to offer a counter-argument, I'd be willing to hear you out.

If a conspiracy involving trafficking girls under the age of consent to some of the world's most powerful people is not permitted to be spoken of in mainstream media, you have to start asking what else is not permitted to be discussed. You have to start wondering how trustworthy are the sources you have entrusted to keep you informed. And you have to begin to realize just how fundamentally corrupt are the media whose job it is to give to you the information you need to participate in a democratic society.

But more than anything, you have to start to realize that what they have you thinking about is not what you should be thinking about but merely a distraction to prevent you from concentrating on what is most relevant to your life. Once you start to realize that everything you have been focusing your attention on your entire adult life, those things that make you unspeakably angry and depressed, are there to distract you from more important issues, you will realize that the media is not and has never been your friend.

Why We Feel We're Alone Or In The Minority

The headline I read today was "Climate concern in Wisconsin is more common than you think". In the article, it says that "up to 90% of Americans underestimate how much people care about climate change". "While 62% worry about climate change and support policies, they believe they are in the minority, thinking that only 42% share the same concerns." "Scientists say that when people think others aren't concerned — or even skeptical — that stops them from talking about their concerns." "'These perceptions are holding people back in terms of expressing that concern, voicing it to others and perhaps organizing around it.'"

Interesting and important reporting. Unfortunately, the only reason provided for why people feel they are in the minority on this issue is that "people have a hard time gauging what the majority believes because often the minority tends to be visible and loud."

It sounds to me that the article is referring to MAGA (Trump supporters). I'm not giving them a pass, but let me suggest another group that is a distinct minority but has the ability to drown out the opinions of others: the media itself. The media, more than any other entity I'm aware of, has the power to fashion the perceptions of the populace. The media has not merely failed to provide us with the relevant information we need regarding climate change, their lies of omission regarding climate change has many of us believing we are in a minority that worries about climate change. Watch the establishment corporate media, read the corporate news sources, and you will see just how little a priority they place on one of the most vital issues of our day.

You can blame MAGA for this if you like, but keep in mind MAGA was raised by the mainstream media, most likely far more than the rest of us. Travel into the heart of MAGA, visit the most destitute and desperate trailer park where Let's Go Brandon flags fly at every lot, and despite whatever else the people there lack, I'm guessing they'll have a satellite dish, antenna, or cable connection. The problem is not that they don't have access to the kind of culture mass media has to provide, the problem is that they do.

It's not just climate change, either. The media makes you feel alone on many issues. That is its job. It wants you to feel isolated and powerless, and maybe a little bit crazy. It wants to make you believe they speak for the masses, that they are your friend, that they are looking out for your best interests. And if you don't agree with them, well you are in a very tiny minority and it's time for you to get your head straight.

We saw this after the death of Jeffrey Epstein, immediately after he predictably died under extraordinarily suspect conditions. The media's response was that it was their job to quell any theories that his death was in the least bit suspicious. The problem was not that a blackmailer died in custody and surveillance cameras weren't working, the problem was that those wacky conspiracy theorists would try to question the official explanation.

Minorities can be treated quite cruelly by those with power. We know this from history and from various examples from the present. The media is fairly good at at least giving lip service to that. But when it comes to people who have a view contrary to the majority, the media affords them little sympathy. If you hold a view that does not jibe with what the majority believe, you are a trouble maker, a problem, a bad person, a threat to the American way. It's okay to hate that kind of minority. It's okay to make that sort of minority person feel bad about themselves. It's okay to make them feel self-conscious, to make them feel that they should keep their inner thoughts and feelings to themselves. There is no dissenter pride month, nor is there a dissenter history month.

The thing is, we dissenters are not in the minority. As is shown in the example of climate change, we are in the majority. It is just that it is the media's job to make us feel as though we are in the minority. And in terms of those who are suspicious of the official narrative regarding the death of Jeffrey Epstein, I'm guessing we are at 95 or so percent. The media will never, EVER, allow us to contemplate that.

The media has its thumb on the scales so that they do not fall from our eyes. Weigh that into every perception you have about whether or not you are in a minority that should be expected to remain silent. Think about that every time you have a thought you feel might separate you from the rest of humanity. It just might be that it is a thought shared by others, a thought they wished someone else might utter so that they would not feel so utterly alone.

Corporate Media Vs. Citizen Journalism

If Mainstream Corporate Journalists and Internet Citizen Journalists were each a collective entity, they would sound something like this:

Mainstream Corporate Journalist: I am a journalist.
Internet Citizen Journalist: I'm just trying to point out facts.

MCJ: I work for a corporation.
ICJ: I work for myself.

MCJ: If I don't earn a profit for my employers, I will be fired and have to get a real job.
ICJ: I already have a real job and will likely never make a penny for my efforts.

MCJ: My money comes from corporate sponsors that include the pharmaceutical industry, the fossil fuel industry, and even military contractors.
ICJ: If I am lucky and do my job well, I will have supporters that throw a few bucks at me on Patreon.

MCJ: The more I speak for the powerful, the more successful I will be.
ICJ: The more I speak truth to power, the more successful I will be.

MCJ: I supported the Iraq War.
ICJ: I opposed the Iraq War.

MCJ I got up on television and said you were basically a traitor to your country if you opposed the Iraq War.(Joe Scarborough)
ICJ: Nevertheless, I went out on a street corner holding a sign opposing the Iraq war while rednecks in a pickup truck with a huge American flag swore at us and threatened us with violence.

MCJ: I said there was no doubt there were WMDs in Iraq.
ICJ: I didn't believe it.

MCJ: I now refer to the Iraq War as a mistake.
ICJ: I now refer to the Iraq War as a crime.

MCJ: I hope that you will forget that I once supported the war so that I can maintain my appearance of having integrity.
ICJ: I hope you will remember that I opposed the war, thus proving my integrity.

MCJ: I work hard at my job in the hopes that one day I will get paid like Rachel Maddow or Sean Hannity.
ICJ: I work hard at my job in the hopes of saving the planet from environmental destruction and nuclear war.

MCJ: I have access to Robert Mueller and Mike Pompeo and am able to ask questions of them and get their responses.
ICJ: I point out how Robert Mueller is a liar and Mike Pompeo is an admitted liar and whatever they say should not be trusted.

MCJ: I have been making people aware of the protests in China.
ICJ: I have been making people aware of the protests in the United States. And Lebanon and Iraq and Equador and Chile and Columbia and Greece and France and…

MCJ: I have been ignoring Cornell West and slandering Dr. Jill Stein.
ICJ: I have been pointing out this bias.

MCJ: I have been saying that Medicare For All is unaffordable.
ICJ: I've been saying that it is less expensive and covers more than our current system.

MCJ: I tell people they have to settle for the lesser of two evils.
ICJ: I've been telling people they have within them the power to change things for the better.

MCJ: I promoted Trump as a celebrity before he got involved in politics.
ICJ: I've never liked Trump.

MCJ: I show images of poor people in countries that are being sanctioned for disobeying Washington.
ICJ: I show pictures of homeless people living in tent cities in the United States.

MCJ: I sometimes mention climate change and ask what we can do about it without affecting our economy.
ICJ: I often mention climate change and say we won't have an economy in a few years if we don't do anything about it.

Internet Citizen Journalist: I speak for the planet and say we must protect it.

Mainstream Corporate Journalist: I speak for the fossil fuel industry and the automotive industry and say we need to power our economy.

ICJ: I speak for journalists and say nobody should go to jail for revealing the truth.
MCJ: I say Julian Assange isn't a real journalist like Rachel Maddow and deserves to rot in prison.

ICJ: I say people need to put aside partisan politics and find ways to work together.
MCJ: I say Republicans are the enemy or the Democrats are the enemy, depending on whether I am working for FOX News or MSNBC.

ICJ: I frequently reference Martin Luther King Jr. and other important thinkers and leaders of history.
MCJ: I frequently reference Kanye West and other celebrities.

ICJ: I'm worried about the influence of money in American politics.
MCJ: I'm worried about the influence a picture of Jesus arm-wrestling the devil has on American politics.

ICJ: I want you to care about safe drinking water for Flint Michigan and elsewhere.
MCJ: I'm interested in letting you know which bottled water is best.

ICJ: I seek to enlighten you.
MCJ: I seek to entertain and titillate you.

ICJ: I want you to feel connected, so that you trust yourself.
MCJ: I want you to feel alienated, so that you trust the television.

ICJ: I want you to feel hopeful.
MCJ: I want you to feel fearful.

ICJ: I want you as a comrade.
MCJ: I want you as a loyal viewer.

ICJ: My voice is being censored.
MCJ: MY VOICE IS BEING AMPLIFIED.

The Media Tells Us Nothing About Navalny, Everything About Itself

(Originally published February 17, 2024. Alexei Navalny died in a Russian prison. This essay was in response to the media's assumptions surrounding his death and was written to point out how independent journalists must hold themselves to far greater standards than the establishment media.)

I'll say about Navalny's death what I said about Seth Rich's and Jeffrey Epstein's: it looks suspicious. That's about all I have for now.

My refusal to mindlessly parrot the assertions of U.S. propagandists will no doubt be taken as proof that I have some sort of agenda. It's true, I do. My agenda is not to reveal myself to be an idiot by speaking up when I don't have any details. Other people, people who are brought onto major news channels to espouse their opinions, don't have to worry about being wrong. They lie all the time. Their lies are proven to be false, and nobody ever challenges them or holds them accountable. That's because they speak for the establishment. That's because they speak for power.

I don't have that luxury. I can't appear on some platform and talk to people less informed than myself and have the establishment cover for me. I only have my record of speaking within my own realm of knowledge and not saying things that may later be proven false. If for some reason I should ever gain any degree of notoriety, I am certain that everything I have written will be combed through and held up as evidence, so I do my best to speak responsibly.

So I'll hold off saying much about the death of Navalny until I learn more on the matter. All I know with any degree of certainty is that Navalny was in a Russian prison and died. That's it. As far as I know, nobody has any more information than that, nor has any halfway responsible news institution claimed more. That by itself is certainly newsworthy, but it hardly merits making claims based simply on the fact that it furthers the establishment narrative.

That doesn't stop the chattering propagandists on social media, the Michael McFauls, Gary Kasparovs, and Anne Applebaums, from stating unequivocally that Putin is directly responsible. I'll share this quote from Boris Johnson as a suitable example of how the death of

Navalny is being spoken of by our political elite: "No one can be in any doubt that Alexei Navalny has been put to death by Vladimir Putin — simply because he had the courage to oppose the Russian tyrant." Hardly the measured response of a responsible statesman. But then, no one in the west can be mistaken for being measured or responsible. As for me, I would never speak so confidently without at least attempting to back up what I say. Never. I have too much respect for my fellow human beings for that.

One might expect a more measured response from the leader of the greatest superpower the world has ever known, or at least one would have expected such a thing in days gone by. Instead, as reported by CNN, "Joe Biden was unequivocal Friday in laying blame on Russian President Vladimir Putin for the reported death of opposition figure Alexey Navalny, saying regardless of the details still to come, 'Make no mistake: Putin is responsible.'"

Saying Putin is responsible shows that Biden is irresponsible. As I recall, no leader of any nation so boldly suggested that Epstein's death was unequivocally the fault of the U.S. government or Massad, despite the fact that both clearly had more interest in silencing Epstein than Putin had in silencing Navalny. People whose job it is to represent a nation should be more diplomatic than that. Hell, people whose job it is to clean toilets should be more reserved in their accusations than that.

I'll tell you one thing, though: the difference between Navalny's death and Rich's and Epstein's is that the main suspect doesn't appear to have a motive.

It's a weird time to go killing off a rival. And when I say rival, I mean an insignificant rival. However much the Western media wishes to portray Navalny as the social conscience of Russia and Putin's main threat, the man was politically of little importance. I would like to hear someone's explanation for why killing Navalny was beneficial to Vladimir Putin. I would argue that it would be a foolish mistake made by someone who doesn't have a track record of making foolish mistakes.

It was the same thing with Sergei Skripal, when he was poisoned. He had previously been held in a Russian prison, was released, and permitted to move to England. Years later, without any sort of motive, Putin is said to have sent (apparently incompetent) agents to kill him using a nerve agent so deadly that it didn't kill the intended victim. This in no way benefited Putin and was used as a major P.R. campaign by the Western media and political class as an excuse to boycott Russia's hosting of the World Cup seven weeks later.

As with the Skripal case, those who appear to make a living telling us we have to fear Russia and that everything bad ever done since the dawn of recorded history is undoubtedly the fault of Putin (hyperbole, but only slightly), the death of Navalny is used to send more money and weapons to Ukraine. My X (Twitter) feed is full of people I don't even follow yelling at the top of their lungs about avenging the death of someone whose greatest attribute is that he permits the West to hate on Russia even more than it already does.

So I'll reserve my judgment on what has happened until we know more than "Navalny has died." Assuredly once saner heads have had time to investigate and more trustworthy voices have had time to speak, we shall be capable of having an intelligent discussion on the matter. In the meantime, get ready for a shitstorm of propaganda from the voices of war and empire.

As Jack London once said, "American journalism has its moments of fantastic hysteria, and when it is on the rampage the only thing for a rational man to do is to climb a tree and let the cataclysm go by."

We Have Replaced Communication With Propaganda (Our Leaders Have Stopped Listening)

I sort of accidentally ended up minoring in communications as a way of doing an internship. It turned out really changing the way I view things, forcing me to look at human interactions in a much more sophisticated way than I previously had. One of the first things I was taught was that communication is a cyclical process. The communicator, having related his message, then looks at his audience and expects feedback. The feedback must be processed and responded to. In other words, communication is not about writing a clear memo, it is an ongoing process between two or more groups. This is healthy — nay, vital — to communities and to relationships.

Propaganda, however, is a one way means of funneling information from top to bottom. Even if the propaganda is not being transmitted by one who is in power, it is transmitted by one who hopes to hold power. Those engaging in propaganda to help build a movement are creating the future structures of a top-down information flow.

Now it is obvious that in an advanced society, experts often need to transmit information in a rather top-down fashion. The amount of information that needs to be imparted to someone receiving a doctorate degree is immense. Obviously someone who is a specialist in a given subject must be given extra magnification for his or her message in times of crisis, so that those who have specifically trained for the moment are able to do their job. But genuine communication must be encouraged congruent with the feeding of information if the student is to one day become not merely a reciter of learned knowledge but someone capable of expanding upon existing knowledge.

In any time other than one of extreme crisis, it is imperative that the principles of communication be adhered to and the use of propaganda minimized. Communication is a crucial aspect of maintaining a democracy. Propaganda is necessary to maintain authoritarianism.

Willingness to engage in honest communication in normal times will give you the legitimacy you need to demand enhanced control in moments of crisis. But what we are seeing now is a moment of crisis where those in charge have not established legitimacy. For decades they have been acting as if we have already been in a moment of crisis where functional communication had to be put on hold. One "crisis" has led to another and another until now we find ourselves in permanent crisis mode. And just like the villagers in the story of the boy who cried wolf, the people have developed crisis fatigue.

Now the wolves are at the door and nobody wants to listen to the propagandists. Meanwhile, the propagandists, having become convinced that they did not need to engage in legitimate communication, no longer feel it is necessary and no longer have the skills to engage in it even if they did.

The great danger of this — and we are seeing it now — is that the ruling class, those who are the primary communicators, no longer listen to anyone besides themselves and have become lost in their own narratives. They have mistaken their own lies for truth. The people are no longer listening to them but they aren't even aware of it, because they long ago stopped looking for feedback from the people. They only listen to themselves and each other. They are a small, elite group that recite narratives completely detached from reality. But being detached from reality themselves, they don't even know it.

Just as decades ago, our leaders stopped caring about the feedback the citizens were sending, so too did they stop caring about the feedback they were receiving from other nations. Mali, Russia, China, Iran and others spoke, but our leaders weren't listening. Instead they fed the world propaganda, because for a time they were powerful enough to get away with it. Our perspective was the only one that mattered. That which we dictated to be truth was the only truth.

We know what happens when communication breaks down. In the case of Russia and the West, it led to war in Ukraine. In the case of the Democratic Party, it led to defeat at the hands of a most unlikely candidate. And there is worse for them to come, far worse, because they are not listening to the people they need to vote for them but only to their own propaganda.

All across our society, necessary lanes of communication have broken down. Politicians can scarce appear in front of the people, and when they do so they communicate in talking points rather than with legitimate conversation. Establishment media has forsaken its principle purpose of questioning power and just nods its head as government spokespersons spew forth their talking points. Social media has taken to censoring, deplatforming, and algorithmically suppressing dissenting voices rather than acknowledging them. You have a problem with YouTube, Facebook, or some other huge corporation? Good luck ever speaking to a real person. Even the local newspaper, which has been bought out by a huge conglomerate and eliminated local staff to increase profits, will not respond to you. All you get is an automated response that says "We value your input."

Those who control the narrative are separated from the people and separated from reality. They live in a rarefied environment that would make even the French nobility cringe. Those who are incapable of listening to us are incapable of speaking for us. As in the case of the boy who cried wolf, it will likely not turn out well for the villagers, but one can hardly blame them for their refusal to listen and respond. But as bad as it will be for the villagers, it will not be as bad for them as it will be for the boy who finally spoke the truth after everyone stopped believing him. What you sow, so shall you reap.

Corporate Capitalism Is At War With Nature, Corporate Media Is At War With Reality

Corporate capitalism is a train running full speed toward a cliff. Whatever brakes the train once had have been stripped from it in order to streamline its forward movement.

We are all passengers on this train, lured aboard by the promise that it would take us where we wanted to go. And it has delivered all it has promised and more, at least for those of us not shoveling the coal. The only problem is, every time we arrive at the station we believed was the promised land, the train just keeps on going. Devices that would have been viewed as technological miracles by our grandparents now clog our landfills because they are last generation technology nobody wants. Thus far, all that we are told would give us happiness ends up being discarded as worthless.

We got on this train not merely because of the material goods corporate capitalism provided us but because we were led to believe such products would bring us happiness. But the happiness achieved by our acquisitions is transitory, leaving in its wake a greater emptiness that must be filled. Each time we acquire a new possession, we are again made unhappy the moment a newer model comes out. Our vehicles are more spacious than prior generations ever would have imagined or even thought to ask for. Our televisions sport larger screens and higher definition than our parents would have thought tasteful for placing in their living rooms. We possess so many toys and gadgets that we have to build or rent storage units for them. Our electronic devices provide us with more ways of amusing and distracting ourselves than ever before. Yet, although such devices leave us no time to dwell upon how we feel, we are dimly aware of a growing discontent in the same way we are dimly aware of the train wheels as they move us further along the tracks towards humanity's doom.

Doom IS the inevitable destination. It is obvious to anyone willing to look out their windows and see what's going on outside our comfortable train compartments. We are using every last possible resource we can get our hands on in order to increase the speed of this runaway train. Somewhere deep within us we know real changes have to be made, but the seats upon which we sit are just so damned comfortable, and reality so very frightening.

If corporate capitalism is a runaway train headed towards the abyss, establishment media are the well-paid attendants who offer us fluffy pillows for a slight fee. They offer to close our blinds for us should we desire to take a nap, offer us unhealthy banquets that leave us lethargic, and provide us with a thousand different escapist movies for us to watch. In all ways, they try to make things pleasant for us, insisting only that we remain in our seats for our own safety. And we must never question where it is we are going. There is no destination, only progress.

Should we ever provide ourselves the quiet moments required for honest reflection, we would be forced to admit some unpleasant but necessary truths. We are depleting our natural resources at a fevered and irrational pace. We destroy nature to create unneeded products we use to reward ourselves in order to numb our anxiety. We devastate our environment in waging endless war against those whose ideologies might impede the advancement of the train that is leading us to our own graves. We waste our energies and creativity in the manufacture of drugs and penitentiaries in order to medicate and imprison those who are unable or unwilling to sit quietly as the train's speed increases. Most of all, we lay waste to nature because it often provides free alternatives to that which corporations wish to sell you.

Nature can provide food without cost. It can provide us with wisdom that even our most prestigious and expensive universities cannot. It gives us opportunities for exercise superior to any treadmill or climbing wall. It can give us an understanding of freedom that a Harley Davidson or maxi-pad never can. It is able to give us a sense of contentment superior to anything pharmaceuticals provide. Sadly, what it cannot do is pay advertisers to advocate for it. Commercials scream, nature whispers.

Corporate capitalism is the reason our climate is quickly being converted to one which is unsuitable for human habitation. Under no circumstances would a corporation want you to use less energy when corporations profit off your energy use. They will never encourage you doing without that which you do not need to begin with because they profit from selling you that which does not make you happy. And if what they have sold you does not make you happy, they have a product that is sold as a cure for that. So the living creatures in our oceans are replaced with plastic particles and oil spills, the wild creatures in our forests and prairies are replaced by caged animals on factory farms. All that is holy, all that is natural, is being replaced by that which is profitable. Corporate capitalism is at war with nature.

As corporate capitalism is at war with nature, corporate media is at war with reality. They call it marketing but it could just as well be called corporate propaganda. There is no other message to be had from our televisions, no alternate way of viewing our situation. Turn on the television and you will not hear one voice speaking out on behalf of nature. Nature has no money to spend on air time. Neither do the poor, the elderly, or the victims of war. All of the power of the media's voice comes from corporations paying to have their message spread.

The choice is becoming starker as the train builds up steam: the planet or the corporations. The train which carries us forward is undoubtedly a remarkable feat of engineering, but there is no longer any reasonable doubt that the ride cannot continue much longer. We must do all that is in our power to stop its hurtling toward its undeniable destination. The seating is undeniably luxurious, but it will not comfort us once the crash occurs. The distraction the media supplies is assuredly pleasant, but on the day the illusion is stripped away, it will not drown out the cries of those in agony from the train wreck. The terminus is far closer than anyone in the media will have you believe.

Learn What Good Writing Looks Like, And You'll Never Look At Mainstream Media The Same Way Again

When you write a lot, and when you put that writing in front of a lot of people's eyes, you start to take a real critical look at what it is you're writing, because you want to make sure people don't read something you didn't intend. You try to look at your writing in ways you imagine other people would look at it, try to imagine how liberals and conservatives, believers and atheists, men AND women might perceive it. It is hard to write honestly without expanding one's perspective, since one is always trying to understand other people's perspectives.

When it finally dawns on you people are actually reading your writing and judging it, you ask yourself before you hit publish whether or not the argument is convincing and whether it is built upon solid facts or merely on conjecture, flimsy evidence, and hearsay.

I'm okay publishing an article that is not firmly built upon facts so long as I make it clear that I am merely laying out a theory that can either be bolstered or weakened by new facts coming to light. And I feel it is useful to occasionally write an article that points out the holes in establishment opinion without being able to prove that it is wrong, just so long as I make clear that is what I am doing. I live quite well with ambiguity and believe others should be able to do so as well. Not everything is known, but drawing in the knowns will eventually help lead to a better understanding. I believe it is quite useful to draw a sketch of what might be the truth using logic and a basic understanding of history and human behavior. Just so I don't try to pass it off as a photograph.

This is what writing a lot has taught me. And in learning to question whether I am following my own simple rules of writing before publishing, I naturally look at the writing of others in the same fashion. What I find in establishment media is shocking.

When I write, the only facts I present are those that have solid evidence that I can share with others. Not evidence that's secret, not evidence that someone showed me but I can't show others. Not evidence based on anonymous informers. I would never expect people to believe me if I were to do such a thing. I respect my readers way too much. More than that, I respect myself and the idea that sifting and winnowing will lead to the most honest and most likely explanations for what is going on in the world.

More than anything, I am quick to apologize for anything I may have gotten wrong. Nobody is perfect and everybody gets the facts wrong or engages in faulty reasoning occasionally. I welcome feedback and the opportunity to correct my mistakes, because it is my reputation that is on the line and nobody cares about my reputation more than I do.

I remember after the Iraq War began when no weapons of mass destruction were found, how the New York Times admitted they were wrong to say with almost absolute authority that they existed and we needed to go to war to prevent them from being used. They said that they had failed their readers and that they would try harder in the future. They never did. In fact, they've gotten much worse in the ensuing decades.

It is my vow to you that should I ever get a story as wrong as the NYT and many other publications did that I will retreat into obscurity and never bother you with my thoughts again. I can't imagine the kind of atonement I might do that would allow me to live with myself for such a failure.

I have written a lot that not only questions the establishment narrative but quite boldly refutes much of what the establishment media says. One of us is wrong. If it can be proven that it is me, prove it and I will slink away. If it cannot be proven that anything of substance I have said is wrong, then you should start heavily tempering what you see in establishment media with what you hear from me and other independent writers, reporters, and journalists who critique official sources. And if we are able to prove to you how the corporate establishment media is not merely wrong on an occasional issue but shows a pattern of being wrong without feeling the need for serious mea culpas and substantive changes, you seriously need to question your relationship with establishment media.

Quite frankly, it should have been done decades ago. It should have been done when every mainstream media outlet led us into a war based on a faulty premise. As Jimmy Dore said, after the Iraq War, your immediate response when they tell you something should be "They're lying". That's all they deserve. That's all anybody deserves when they tell you something of such import that is so far from reality. You need to demand tangible proof, not the unproven allegations of anonymous sources. They lied and people died. That has consequences and you are complicit in that lie so long as you continue to follow them. If it wasn't a lie, it sure was a massive, MASSIVE, failure.

They don't deserve your trust. They should be working as hard as they can to show you that they are worthy of regaining your trust. They're not. They're giving you unsubstantiated reporting and DARING you not to believe them. You deserve better from them, and the world deserves better from you.

I don't deserve your trust, either. I'm working as hard as I can to earn it, by speaking as honestly and digging as deeply into the evidence available to me as I can. Don't trust me, read what I write critically. But do not dismiss me or others like me simply because the establishment media has you afraid of those who do not uncritically agree with what it is they are feeding you. It is they, and no one else, who have the blood of millions on their hands. It is they, not we, who live rich on money they receive from the corporations that profit at the expense of the people.

Establishment media will never tell you anything that will cost the arms manufacturers, the big banks, Blackrock, Monsanto, Exxon Mobil, Comcast, and other transnational corporations a penny.

Go ahead, prove me wrong.

Trust Is A Gift You Give, Not Something Others Can Demand Of You

Calm yourself. For it is when you are at peace that you can perceive things as they are. War is the murder of peace and when peace is no more, your perception of reality dissolves into madness. With a world dedicated to war and domination, reality itself is shifted. All that once was clear is swept away, so that the only truth remaining is the pronouncements of the powerful.

Those who shout are looking to roil the placid waters, trying to make it impossible for anyone either to peer beneath the surface or to reflect upon oneself. They wish you to see only the turmoil, which is ever-changing and impossible to understand. Then they will tell you they are scryers capable of interpreting the unfathomable.

Breathe. Find your center, find yourself. Find that truth within you that reverberates with external truth, so that you are capable of making your own decisions. Trust the experts if you choose, but do not do so out of fear or from coercion. Do not lightly place your trust in people, but allow yourself to first ask yourself if their arguments are in harmony with what your body and your mind are telling you. Those who speak the truth should not be setting off any warning bells within you. Those who speak the truth should not be demanding you agree with them but rather be confident enough in their own truth that they will argue their points calmly and rationally. Those who speak the truth, rather than insisting that you would agree, would rather move on to someone more receptive to truth should you reject them.

Trust, if you like, but remember that trust is a gift you give to another, a gift that no one has the right to demand of you. Trust authority, if trusting is your choice. But do so conditionally, as you should trust anyone. Just as anyone should assume that they must earn your trust, so too should they expect that they must maintain your trust. If they do not receive your trust as a sacred gift, they are unworthy of it.

If you trust in another and your trust is betrayed, this betrayal must be addressed before you ever place your trust in that person or that institution again. Apologies devoid of meaningful change are the most obvious sign that your trust will be abused by that person or institution for as long as you continue to trust them. We are living in a world of insincere apologies today, a world where professional crisis teams guide the untrustworthy through the process of regaining trust without meaningfully changing anything about themselves.

We tend to give our trust to the untrustworthy when we are afraid of being on our own. We give our trust to the unworthy because we have not yet learned to trust ourselves, our own decision-making processes and our own inner voice. Our own insecurities are like unlocked doors through which the untrustworthy impose themselves into our personal space.

If we wish to gain control of the power to trust or withhold trust, we must learn how to be comfortable being alone. We must learn to trust our own perceptions even if it sometimes requires us to be separate from the herd. We must learn to trust ourselves, and to do that we must first learn to listen to ourselves. To do that, we must learn to be calm, so that we permit the various voices within us to be heard. To do so, we must learn to embrace peace, which means seeing and relating to things as they are, without the desire to control. For the moment we feel the need to be in control, we will realize how completely unable we are to control the outside world. And then those who promise us they can control the outside world will ask us to trust them to do so. And we will do so, because we believe that in this way we have some degree of control by proxy. Then, not only will we not be in control of the outside world, we will no longer be in control of ourselves.

Breathe. Calm yourself. Hear yourself. Feel yourself. Be yourself. In this way you will be at peace even as you begin to gain power over the one thing you truly can control: yourself. The alternative is madness and manipulation.

The Establishment Doesn't Respect You, It's Up To You To Respect Yourself

The media does not respect you. It tells you the sort of lies a child would tell while assuming the authority of a parent.

Your politicians do not respect you. They tell you what you want to hear when they need your vote, then they pass the laws their donors want them to pass.

The corporations you work for do not respect you. They tell you that you are part of a family and then let you go the moment you are no longer of use to them.

The artists do not respect you. Art should elevate your thoughts and emotions to the stars, but they drag you down into the dirt.

Why do you give them your approval to run things, to speak for you and interpret the world for you? Is it because for now things are tolerable and the risk that things could get worse is real? Is it because you believe that they might see the error of their ways and voluntarily reform themselves to be who you want them to be? If you allow yourself to believe YOUR rationalizations, it is because you've already allowed yourself to believe THEIR rationalizations.

Their lies are ever more obvious, their promises becoming ever more empty, their art becoming ever more vapid and vulgar, their business dealings becoming ever more one-sided and openly ruthless.

Their contempt for you is becoming ever more apparent.

Their conviction of their own worth is ever more deluded.

Their disregard for anything other than their own ego gratification is becoming ever more revolting.

You have to do something.

You have to step out from the limitations they have built for you.

You have to take one timid little step just to reassert your humanity, to show that you are not entirely and utterly obedient.

Something.

Anything.

You have to believe there is some small area of your life that is not being monitored by their cameras, that is not being recorded by their computers, some small little spot in this big world where you are able to spread what is left of your wings in order to feel like a human being again. I am reluctant to use the word because it is so overused and misused, but there must be something inside of you that yearns for freedom. That yearns to be self-directed rather than be directed by external forces. There is something inside you still that is you, that is something more than what other people have told you you have to be.

Something sacred.

There is something better than the dystopian future they are herding you towards. There has to be. Dare to tear yourself away from the machine for a moment, dare to breath the air as you were meant to, and you will know it.

What The TV Wants Me To Think

I'm beginning to think my TV wants me to hate Russia.
Not just a little, either. A lot.
I'm beginning to think my TV wants me to ignore Yemen
And to think Israel is always good. Always.
I think my TV wants me to believe that Julian Assange is not a journalist.
Why else would all the handsomely paid journalists on TV not rush to his aid?
I think my TV wants me to believe that anyone without a corporate media contract shouldn't be able to express their views at all.
That it's everyone else's job just to parrot what they've heard from the media.
I think they want me to believe that people shooting cars into space are going to save the environment.
That billionaires owning everything will be good for small businesses.
That voting for the slightly lesser evil is the highest good.
I think it wants me to believe we're building back better by shipping weapons to Ukraine,
and that this is not a proxy war.

I think they want me to think that they would never lie
to us
That they want what's best for us
That the highest forms of proof are the assertions of
unnamed intelligence agents.
I think they want us to believe Madeline Albright is a
good role model for young girls
At least the ones that weren't killed by the sanctions
she supported.
I really think the TV wants us to believe there was
nothing weird about Jeffrey Epstein's death
Or Hunter Biden's appointment to a Ukrainian energy
company.
I think they are trying to make us believe Joe Biden isn't
having age-related cognitive issues
And that there is some actual substance to Kamala
Harris.
I think they want us to believe that AOC is going to raise
a ruckus
That her dress was empowering to the working class.
I think the media wants us to believe that sometimes
you have to risk a nuclear war
And that not all Nazis are bad.
I'm starting to think the TV wants me to believe that
every expression of dissent is Russian propaganda.
I'm starting to feel the TV doesn't want me to think that
China will be their next target.
I'm starting to think the TV doesn't want me to think at
all.
I think it wants me to believe that we need to be told
what to think.
That war is peace and truth is lies

When necessary.
I think the media wants me to laugh or be outraged when it tells me to.
I'm beginning to suspect they want me to buy stuff
That it'll make me happy.
That happiness is found in a pill or a car payment.
That love cannot be expressed without a diamond
That my six-year-old needs a smart phone.
I think they want me to buy my water in single-use plastic containers.
I think they want me to think all that plastic just disappears.
I think they want us to think that Ellen DeGeneres can be George Bush's buddy and ours, too.
I think the talking heads want us to believe they can work for billionaires and still be on our side.
I think they want us to believe without ever giving us the facts we need to make up our own minds.
I think I shall resist another day.

Time To Abandon A Sinking Narrative

As the official narratives drift further and further from reality, which way will you go? Will you cling to the illusion of comfort and safety official narratives provide you, or will you allow yourself to drift back toward your natural inclinations, toward what common sense, your own observations, and your own sense of health are telling you? Will you continue to listen to the person on TV being paid $30,000 a day who has no idea what your daily life is like? Will you continue to bow to their authority and their greater wisdom when all around you life is continually getting worse?

Know that if you are about to take the leap that you will not be alone. Our numbers are already rather impressive, and we are not going back. We will never again allow ourselves to rejoin the meta-reality created by the media after stepping out from under it. It is not the all-pervasive entity we once thought, it is merely a dark theater playing absurdist films to a stultified audience.

We see the environmental degradation and we know the media will never report on it and our politicians will never meaningfully act on it. We see the rank corruption in both of our political parties and we know that Joe Biden and Donald Trump are the best this system will ever give us. It's just going to get worse from here, folks. We see the wealth of our nations — as President Eisenhower warned us 62 years ago — being spent on weapons of destruction. We see the unreality of the confused, psychotic narrative that is unable to maintain continuity from one day to the next.

We await you. Eagerly. Freed from the illusions of the narrative machine, we are nonetheless imprisoned by the consequences of its operations so long as a majority of the people give it credence and support. We cannot do this without you. We, perhaps more clearly than anyone else, realize how interdependent we all are and how we are all in this together.

I think the sticking point so many of you have is your unwillingness to admit that the media is agenda driven, not truth driven. Within the media, the truth is twisted, ignored, slandered, and censored a thousand times a day in order to advance the prime directives of profit and dominance. But people don't want to see it. Unless, of course, it is the murdering of truth that takes place on the other side of the political spectrum. That, they see perfectly clearly. Then they see how brazenly the reporters and the politicians lie and how eagerly their audience consumes the lies. But the media on the left and the media on the right have 95% of the same agenda, they merely justify it by different means. FOX News and MSNBC can spout the most virulent hatred towards the other, but neither side addresses the fact that Flint Michigan doesn't have clean drinking water. Nobody is showing the homeless crisis not only in Los Angeles but all across our country. Nobody ever points a critical camera at the people who donate to both parties and benefit no matter who wins.

The media is paid for by the machinery and will never criticize the machine. It is therefore evident that the media will never protect our planet against the machinery that profits off its destruction. The media is not sponsored by trees, it is sponsored by those who see in trees nothing more than the profit that can be made by their destruction. The media is not paid for by the animals that are killed by the oil spills and the factory farms and the pollution and the over-harvesting of mega fishing boats. The machine doesn't factor in human survival, so why should it care about other species?

We are at a critical tipping point now. The moment is desperate, but this very desperation will cause the necessary numbers to flee from the sinking ship that is the media illusion. Judging by the numbers garnered by true independent media outlets, we already number around a million. We are never going back, never returning to the fold, so don't expect things will go back to normal. Things are never going back to normal, nor should they. The future lies beyond the floundering vessel that sinks under the weight of its outmoded narrative. We who sit at the edge of the impending catastrophe call to you, knowing that we will sink or swim together, that our fates are inextricably intertwined. I have no doubt we will all be sucked in by its wake should we not distance ourselves from it.

This is a call to action for those of you who are free of the media matrix, too. It is not enough to merely be awake, you need to get out of bed and go about the business of creating something others would want to wake up to. Start building alternatives, don't wait for something to happen. You are the early adapters. It is up to you to not merely weave new narratives, you must also show that you are able to live by them. Be bold, be brave, but more than anything, see the beauty and the possibility that can be woven from the current crisis.

Where Have All The Trusted Voices Gone?

I listened to former editor of Harper's Magazine, Lewis Lapham, on Loud And Clear a while ago. I remember 20 years ago reading his work, but somehow I lost track of him over the years. He was of course brilliant, because he is always brilliant. Which got me to thinking about why I haven't heard from him of late. Then it struck me: I was listening to him on Sputnik radio, a Russian-backed radio outlet. And every person I especially admired 20 years ago, if they were still around, were available to me now on RT (formerly Russia Today) and Sputnik: Dennis Kucinich, Ralph Nader, Greg Palast, Noam Chomsky, Cornel West, John Pilger, Roger Waters, Ralph Nader, and just about anyone I could think of. Conversely, all those voices I once heard on NPR or PBS, albeit rarely, have been completely silenced in U.S. media.

Of course, Sputnik IS propaganda. It is propaganda in the same sense that Russian radio broadcasting dissenting German voices in Hitler's Germany would have been propaganda. In the same way Russian radio broadcasting German voices in Weimar Germany would have been propaganda had they done so. Yet, from all accounts from people I respect like Lee Camp, RT never tells him what to say or what to think.

Not too long ago I heard Chris Hedges and Cornell West discussing 19th Century Russian literature, specifically Dostoyevski's Notes From Underground. On RT. I never heard anything like it on U.S. media. Ever. The closest I can come to this would have been an Aldous Huxley interview I saw on YouTube that was originally from a 1960s 60 Minutes. But nothing from my lifetime. I can only imagine what hearing something like this when I was younger might have meant to me. Something I could have chanced upon between episodes of Charlie's Angels and Love Boat. Something that would have made me feel not completely alienated from the culture in which I lived.

I recently saw Time Magazine's 2002 co-person of the year on CNN, whistleblower Colleen Rowley. Just kidding, I heard her on Sputnik Radio, where she's a regular guest. There was a time I might have heard her on Wisconsin Public Radio. Just to see what they were talking about there nowadays I turned the dial. The subjects discussed were Dog Cancer, Finding Fish That's Safe To Eat, and Help For People Starting Restaurants. I didn't have the heart to explore further.

As I stated recently, I've long been a fan of Jeff Cohen, founder of FAIR (Fairness and Accuracy In Reporting). It was not too long ago I used to watch Jeff Cohen on the FOX news program, Fox News Watch, where they gave feedback on news coverage of important events. FOX News! Now he is persona non grata on U.S. media. The media has no room for someone who critically evaluates the media anymore.

You can hear Jeff on Sputnik's By Any Means Necessary. I did a YouTube search and I couldn't find any clips of Jeff Cohen on any major American media of late, though I did find Jeff Cohen, the actor who played Chunk in The Goonies. I also found a clip from Fox News where a Dr. Jeff Cohen talks about colorectal screening. But if you want any kind of critique of U.S. media, you're going to have to go to Sputnik or RT.

This is how bad U.S. media has become. Don't let them try to blame it on anyone else. Don't believe it when they try to make you fear independent voices. Don't permit yourself to believe that those with integrity yesterday are now traitors to their country. They are speaking the truth, as they have always done. They are just no longer permitted to do so in the United States. Truth has become anathema here.

I make no judgment good or bad about RT or Sputnik except to say that if you want to hear America's voices of conscience from years past you can find them there. And quite a few people of integrity of the present, as well. Does it make me a traitor to say such things? What's important to me is that I'm showing loyalty to those people of integrity and courage who inspired me in my past.

I don't expect corporate media to embrace me anytime soon.

While Epstein's Ties To Powerful Figures Were Being Ignored, The Intercept Was Busy Investigating MAGA's Social Media Posts

(Originally shared on Medium on August 31, 2021)

The mob that flooded Washington D.C. on January 6 of this year are not my people. Even putting politics aside, I'm guessing our taste in food and music and cinema are quite different. And, not to judge a group by its worst members, I imagine them to be untidy, rude, and all-around unpleasant.

And yet, I would gladly invite the whole lot of them over to my house for a backyard barbeque rather than associate with the Epstein crowd. I'd even...I'd even let them choose the tunes.

Who is the Epstein crowd, you ask? I can only speculate who they all may be, not being privy to all the facts of the matter, but I have strong suspicions. It's pretty clear in my mind at least that Prince Andrew, Bill Clinton, former Governor Bill Richardson, and Bill Gates were way chummier with the guy when he was alive than they're claiming now. Various prominent politicians and people with wealth and power also have suspicious and unexplained ties to the man. Worst of all, ties between Epstein and intelligence agencies both domestic and foreign seem quite likely.

I don't like to delve too far into conjecture, but I have to think the level of media silence surrounding those who might have connections to Epstein implies there are some powerful people or institutions that would be embarrassed, to say the least, should those connections come to light. Because even if the whole Epstein story is a big nothing burger, it's one hell of a juicy nothing burger. That the media is claiming they're not covering it because they're above salacious rumor-mongering is the single biggest example of rank hypocrisy I can imagine at the moment. The same news outlets that speculated endlessly about Russian prostitutes pissing on Donald Trump are above suggesting possible connections to Epstein? Please.

No, somebody, even if it was just Entertainment Tonight, would be all over this story unless there was a good reason for them not to be.

The Intercept is the news outlet that is perhaps most well-known for doing adversarial journalism. That was the mission statement they were founded on in 2013, back when Glenn Greenwald helped found it. Glenn Greenwald has since left (some say was pushed out), but the Intercept still likes to boast that they have stayed true to their roots. They of any outlet should be revealing the connections powerful people and institutions had to Jeffrey Epstein. They've had a reputation for digging into stories other outlets won't touch.

Instead, the Intercept has been digging into the social media posts of Gab users in the hopes of finding extremists who might execute another poorly planned hillbilly siege of our nation's capital. Not only are they diving into posts by Cletus and Billy Bob in the hopes of discovering some nefarious plot to overthrow the government between references to the Duke Boys and enjoinders to "Git-R-Done!", since there is so much available data for them to go through, they are making requests for donations and volunteers so they can, er, git-r-done. One of the nation's premier investigative news teams, funded by a billionaire, is asking for your time and money to investigate the social media posts of rednecks.

Meanwhile, an Ecosia search of recent Intercept articles on people and institutions with connections to Epstein and a world-wide underage sex networking ring comes up empty.

All indications are that Epstein's game was blackmail. As Kim Iverson pointed out on her Rockfin channel, the fact that he was connected to so many politicians suggests the blackmailing was not done for money but for political influence. No less a respected journalist than Seymour Hersh called Epstein's cohort's father a Mossad agent, and while Ghislaine Maxwell's father took him to court over it, Hersh won out. It has also been reported that Alex Acosta, the man responsible for Epstein's initial lenient prison sentence, claimed that he was told Epstein belonged to intelligence and was "above his (Acosta's) pay grade". When asked to confirm or deny he said it, Acosta did neither.

If you are reading this and thinking to yourself, "Why should I listen to this guy, he's not a reporter?" I would agree. I'm not a reporter. I don't have the time to do justice to the questions I ask. But the sad fact is, there are no reporters from the "approved" news sources looking into this. This is a story that is important to many, a story with many questions that need answering, a story that looks to incriminate many powerful people and institutions should it be fully told. The fact that nobody is doing the work indicates just how powerful these people and institutions really are.

What Kind Of Journalist WOULDN'T Want To Investigate The Epstein Story?

Imagine being a journalist and not wanting to dig into the Epstein case. It's like a child not wanting to take a peek at the Christmas gifts sitting under the

Christmas tree. It's like a bloodhound not wanting to follow a scent. It's like a gossip not wanting to hear about her neighbor's affair. How could you call anyone a journalist who didn't want to know more about this story?

What traits would you associate with a journalist more than curiosity and a desire to dig for the truth? Oh, sure, they need to do so carefully and diligently, but the overwhelming quality you would associate with a journalist would have to be the desire to get to the bottom of a story, right?

Of course, each journalist has their own beat they're covering, so it's not like every journalist would be expected to cover a story about an international sex ring involving underage girls. But they would all be interested in the number one story of our time. They would all be working on the stories they're involved in, but they would surely gather around to discuss the story that overshadows every other story. Wouldn't they? As they sat at their desks or gathered together for a daily briefing, surely this would be the subject of conversation. Surely everybody would be questioning their editor and whoever was covering this story about the breaking news. Right?

My time in a newsroom was brief and modest. But anyone who's encountered a newsroom, even in fiction, would have some kind of understanding of what a job in a newsroom is supposed to be like. If you've watched Murphy Brown or Mary Tyler Moore or if you've read Superman or Spiderman comics, you have some inkling of what a reporter's job is. And that is to get a scoop on a story that captures the interest of everyone. And this is it, people, this is the story of all-time. This isn't just a global pedophile ring, it's worse. Let me repeat myself, this is WORSE THAN A GLOBAL PEDOPHILE RING. Hard to imagine something worse than that, huh? But it is. It must be, because all the major media companies wouldn't keep quiet about a global pedophile ring. Even the global oligarchy wouldn't be averse to throwing a couple of pedophiles to the masses to appease their sense of justice, even if it was a former president who served the oligarchy well in his time.

IF it was just about child sex slaves. JUST. ABOUT. CHILD SEX SLAVES. Get your mind around that. There is something worse and that is the reason the media is so silent about it. That is THE ONLY reason they would be silent about this. It certainly isn't because they're covering anything more important. Think of the top stories of the last four years and think what could be worse than a child sex slave ring. MSNBC is willing to speculate on Russian prostitutes peeing on Trump based on no evidence and yet they're willing to remain silent when it comes to his involvement with Epstein which is indisputable due to multiple photos of the two hanging out. Dear sweet Jesus, what does it take for Rachel Maddow to keep from making terrible insinuations about Trump? Whatever it is, it's bigger than her Trump Derangement Syndrome. Let me repeat myself, this is BIGGER THAN RACHEL MADDOW'S TRUMP DERANGEMENT SYNDROME.

It's even bigger than corporate media's desire for ratings (read profits). One would be excused for thinking there was nothing bigger than corporate media's desire for ratings. MSNBC's ratings have been tanking since Trump left office. Why wouldn't Rachel open the door to conjecture about Trump's connections to Epstein? It would guarantee her a ratings bonanza. But this is bigger than ratings. Let me repeat myself, the need to keep the silence around Epstein is BIGGER THAN RATINGS.

That's huge. HUGE!!!

A Message To Those Who Say The Media Cannot Be Trusted

A message to those who say the media cannot be trusted:

I agree.

But you must realize the media has already shaped you, don't you? You were raised by the media, and so were your parents. I see its imprint all over you. In your brand loyalty, in your misguided patriotism, in your complete ignorance of other cultures, in your arrogance in thinking you know it all. These are all traits you developed from swimming in a culture immersed in the media's messaging.

I see it in the way you've come to accept bottled water as normal. I see it in the way you never stop to think what happens after you throw something you so desperately needed in the garbage, or after the war you so feverishly supported leaves a foreign nation in ruins. I see it in the toxins you've come to accept as food and in the debt you've been talked into accumulating. I see it in the too big vehicle you don't need and in the newest iPhone you can't afford.

I see it in your admiration for Ronald Reagan, a complete media creation. I saw it when you played Contra and I see it as you wait for the next Call Of Duty video game. I see it in your fear of socialism and single payer health care. My Canadian aunt was in a news piece on the Canadian health care system and I can tell you what a slant the media put on it.

You got your values and your biases from WWE. You are a walking, talking product of a media campaign that was designed to turn you into a slogan-repeating supporter of war and mindless consumption. I can spot it on you a hundred yards off. Your attitudes, your musical tastes, it all comes from the media. The catchphrases you repeat, like "What happens in Vegas stays in Vegas" or "Can you hear me now?" The smell of Mountain Dew and Arby's oozing from your pores, and the smell of Doritos wafting from your breath.

It doesn't matter if you say you don't believe the media. It owns you whether you realize it or not. Rush Limbaugh and Ayn Rand are every bit as much served up by the media as are Barack Obama and CNN, you're just part of a different marketing segment. It feeds your outrage every bit as much as Rachel Maddow has her liberal audience convulsing in hatred over Donald Trump and Vladimir Putin. It feeds your hatred and fear of your fellow human beings so that you can no longer see them as anything but the enemy. JUST LIKE RACHEL DOES.

It drives you to work so many hours for so little spiritual reward that you simply have to find someone to blame for your unhappy life when you've sacrificed so much. The media convinces you to play by the rules and then provides you with a scapegoat when playing by the rules doesn't work.

You can't just turn off the TV now and hope to make it better. Just like you can't just stop talking to your parents and expect their influence on you to stop. They've become a part of you. Their voices speak inside your own mind, whether you acknowledge it or not. It is the same with the media.

If you claim the media is lying, good on you. If you believe you are immune to the influence of the media, you are more fooled than anyone. You want to free yourself and the world from the influence of the media? It's going to take a lot of time and effort. You're going to have to do a lot of self-work, because every time you open your mouth its like the TV is talking.

You will never be free until you begin to understand how much your mind has been shaped by an entity more all-pervasive than any religion or government has been before. It was teaching you before you could speak, before you could stand. It was teaching you when your parents were too busy to give you their time because they were doing what the media told them they should be doing.

You've got a glimpse of how the media lies. Good. But don't tell others the media is lying until you do the work required to understand how the media has lied to YOU.

The Four Fallacies Surrounding Conspiracy Theories

At the opposite end of the spectrum from the aluminum foil hat wearing conspiracy theorists are those who believe without question everything authority tells them. Neither group is to be swayed by facts, logic or argument. They will be especially impervious to persuasion from anyone outside of the group they identify with.

One group believes because it fits their narrative of the world. The other group is fearful of questioning official narratives because it might force them to change their comfortable way of life.

Between the two extremes is a vast area that allows for questioning of authority while giving respect to those who have spent their lives pursuing their chosen areas of expertise. In the middle can be found the position that sometimes people with a desire for power conspire to advance certain narratives for their own benefit at the expense of society at large. It's hardly a radical notion.

There are four different errors that people can make regarding conspiracy theories. The first is automatically believing that all conspiracy theories are false. The second is, upon becoming convinced that one conspiracy does exist, subscribing to every conspiracy theory that comes along. The third is becoming so lost and confused by the myriad details that one abandons the search for truth altogether. The fourth is mistaking a theory for a conviction rather than a working hypothesis.

The media would have you make the first error: believing that there is no such thing as a conspiracy. If you disbelieve in conspiracy theories, that means everything the media tells you is truth and there is no reason to question anything they tell you. They do their best to smear anyone who says anything contrary to the official narrative as an unhinged nutjob incapable of grasping the obvious truth.

Much of the fringe-right media would have you commit the second error: being convinced that every conspiracy they feed you is gospel truth. Although they act as if they are combating the mainstream media by presenting alternative narratives, they are actually supporting the mainstream media by acting as the bad example. The mainstream media merely has to point to an Alex Jones to show how crazy conspiracists are. Thus Alex Jones is able to speak truth from time to time, because whatever truth he might utter will be dismissed as the rantings of a maniac. Which he more or less is. And of course, they use people like Alex Jones to represent even those who intelligently question official narratives. Those who spread unsourced, easily disproven memes on social media are also doing the work of the mainstream media, though they believe in their hearts that they are doing their best to oppose it. In making themselves out to be brave proponents of the truth, they cast a poor light upon those who've invested many hours of their lives critically assembling pertinent facts.

The end goal is to have people fall into the third error: becoming so disheartened by the immense amount of information and disinformation available to them that they give up hope of finding out what is true and what is not. It's impossible to hide the truth forever, but it is relatively easy to gather so many half-truths about it that you no longer recognize the real truth when you see it.

If I may indulge in a conspiracy theory for a moment, I would say there is a healthy disinformation campaign taking place on social media these days that seeks to muddy the waters behind certain issues. I would add that this is so pervasive that people lose interest in ever finding the truth. There are those who seek to sow discord among conservatives and liberals, and I'm not talking about Russia. I cannot provide evidence for all that I suggest, nevertheless I can supply you with enough facts of similar disinformation campaigns to show it is not only logical but likely that much worse than what I can prove is occurring. A read of Trust Us, We're Experts by Sheldon Rampton and John Stauber will provide you with ample evidence of corporate manipulation of facts and the use of astroturfing (groups that seem to be grassroots but are actually well-funded marketing firms) to sway public opinion. A quick read-up on The Church Committee and Cointelpro will show you how our country's intelligence agencies are every bit as active as corporations in trying to get you to believe the narratives that suit them best. From there, it is not difficult to extrapolate that many of the people you may come across on the internet are not real people with real opinions but narrative control agents.

The fourth error is the one area in which we have the most control. We do not have all the resources, the reach, or the time necessary to take on official narratives pushed by the establishment media. We do not have the time to shoot down every crackpot theory advanced by the loony fringe types who will only answer your cogent arguments with vitriol and an unwillingness to be held to facts. We cannot clear the waters that trolls and astroturfers are intent on roiling. We can only fight the attempts at narrative control by continuing to question official narratives in critical ways. We do not have to accept any given conspiracy theory as either definitely real or definitely false. We merely need to question what is questionable and acknowledge what is undeniable. We don't have to change people's opinions, we just have to remind them how the pursuit of truth is best conducted. In short, we don't have to make anybody believe anything, we simply have to make people realize it is okay to think outside of the parameters set for them.

It's called tolerance for ambiguity. It's called critical thinking. It's called being a free thinker. It's called intellectual humility. It's being unafraid to say, "I'm not sure."

Authority is important, but it is precisely because it is so crucial to have respected authorities in society that unscrupulous people will attempt to don the guise of authority. It is why people with power and ambition will forever seek to exert pressure on those with authority to change or soften their message. We must never place authority above question. Indeed, it is the very sign of legitimate authority that it would never expect to be placed above suspicion. It has always been my experience that those with a passion for a field of study large enough for them to make it their life's work are more than willing to discuss issues with you and help clarify that which seems unclear.

It is those who insist you accept their authority rather than their explanations who will try to shut down conversation on an issue. They will make the options very simple (though wrong), insisting that there are two extremes to choose from with no room for honest discussion. It's called shutting down conversation and dissent.

It is quite possible to go through life without holding definitive positions on any given subject. In fact, I would say it is necessary. You must learn to respond to reality while seeing through more than one perspective, even knowing that if one is true, the other will be false. Because certainty can be dangerous, and it is always wise to mitigate risk in a world where things are never very certain.

If you outright dismiss narratives that run contrary to the official version, you are helping foster an atmosphere where drawing outside the lines is frowned upon. If you too readily accept narratives outside the official ones, you are making those who intelligently dissent from official narratives look stupid. In either case, you are hindering society's ability to find its way closer to the truth. Do not choose either extreme, not because they are extreme but because they demand simplistic answers and are incapable of nuanced thinking.

The Public Isn't Interested In A Sex Trafficking Scandal Involving Presidents And The Royal Family (An Imagined Newsroom Conversation)

A young reporter rushes into the editor's office.

Reporter: I've got a great story, Ed. This one's got it all. It's got sex, it's got kidnapping, it's got international intrigue. It's got compelling human drama. Best of all, it's got really huge names attached to it. It's got everything you can imagine.

Editor: Calm down, Joe. Let's approach this carefully. You might be on to something but we need to game plan this. The first question we ask in journalism is "who". Are there any politicians involved? Even tangentially? They don't have to be directly involved but we could use a known name in the headlines to get people's interest.

Reporter: I'll say it has politicians involved! Not just politicians, actual FREAKING Presidents of the United States.

Editor: Can it be confirmed by anonymous sources from any intelligence agencies?

Reporter: It's better than that, Ed. Something actually happened. Like there's actually tangible verifiable evidence. Actual witnesses. Real live people. There are pictures. Of the current president! Standing next to an actual international sex trafficker. Plus, flight logs showing a former president actually flew on the sex trafficker's private plane! Dozens of times!

Editor: Any connection to Putin?

Reporter: Well, no...But even better! We've got a member of the Royal Family involved in this. You know how people love any scandal involving the Royal Family. This is going to be crazy huge!

Editor: This member of the Royal Family, has he been to Russia in the last few years?

Reporter: Uh...I don't know. Anyway, forget about him for now. This sex trafficker, he's got ties to Bill Gates. Bill Freaking Gates!

Editor: I don't know, Joe. I've got to go with my gut on this one and I'm not feeling any heat about this story. I want you to follow up on the Russian spy porpoises story. Any new leads on that?

Reporter: Nobody cares about the Russian spy porpoise story, Ed. People thought it was stupid. I was embarrassed to have my name attached to it. Besides, only Democratic voters cared about it at all. This story about the international sex trafficker, now, EVERYBODY will want to know about this. Doesn't matter if you're a Republican or a Democrat or third party. It doesn't matter if you're not even into politics. And the best part, Ed, the best part is that nobody else is covering it. We've got this scoop all to ourselves. All we have to do is a little digging.

Editor: Sorry, I just don't think the public is interested in tawdry stories like this. Our readers are too sophisticated to get pulled into something so lurid.

Anything breaking on the possible existence of videos of Russian prostitutes peeing on Trump?

Reporter: Ed, there's been nothing new on that story in the last four years. There never was any evidence, it was just rumor. But it's indisputable that something really happened with this story. All we have to do is a little digging and we are certain to find gold.

Editor: Sounds a little too "dog bites man" to me.

Reporter: Are you kidding me?

Editor: Trust me, I've been in the news business for twenty years. I've seen this kind of story come across my desk every few months.

Reporter: No, you haven't. And I'm not going back to the last assignment you gave me about Russian agents sowing discord on Instagram by promoting sex toys. I'm telling you, this story has legs and it's going to be huge. We've got to run with it.

Editor: I don't know, maybe you're seeing something I'm not. Is there an angle I'm missing here?

Reporter: I didn't even have a chance to tell you the really crazy part. This international billionaire sex trafficker who's tied to hugely rich and influential people? He seemingly was allowed to kill himself before the truth could come out. It's like Ruby killing Oswald except the cameras weren't working this time.

Editor: You say he killed himself?

Reporter: Allegedly.

Editor: But there wasn't any video of him doing it, like with Trump and the Russian prostitutes?

Reporter: I don't think there's any video of that either. But there was supposed to be two video cameras monitoring his cell and neither one was working.

Editor: Any of the guards see anything?

Reporter: The guards were negligent and didn't check on the prisoner like they were supposed to.

Editor: Wait a minute...I think I see an angle, a way we could make this a story worth reporting on.

Reporter: You let me know boss, and I'll start digging into it.

Editor: Right. Okay, got it. I want you to see how independent journalists and people on social media are covering this and we can do a story about how quick conspiracy theories start.

Reporter: Right away boss! Wait...What?!

An Evening Watching MSNBC

(Originally shared on March 22, 2021)

MSNBC Host: Intelligence officials today said they have determined that Russia did undetermined bad things. For more on this, let me bring on a guest who has spent her entire career in the intelligence community. Welcome Josephine McCarthy. Josephine, can you confirm for me that Russia did unspecified bad things?

Josephine: I spoke to someone in the intelligence community today and he confirmed for me that Russia did indeed do unspecified things that were bad.

MSNBC Host: Well, I guess that question has been answered. Could you give the audience any example of a thing the Russians did that was bad?

Josephine: The agency cannot confirm any specific thing happened, but they have assured me that things were done, Russians did them, and the things done were bad things.

MSNBC Host: Shocking! When we return from our commercial break, we'll talk to a security expert about how we can protect people on social media from hearing untrue ideas.

Commercial: Raytheon. Making the world safe, one drone strike at a time.

Commercial: MSNBC, providing you in-depth news coverage to help you understand the world in which we live.

Commercial: Are you experiencing side-effects from the prescription medication Controll, commonly used to alleviate the side-effects of the drug Pacifex? Ask your doctor if Neutrol might be right for you. From the makers of Zombien and Blissoquil.

MSNBC Host: Welcome back. As of late there have been a lot of fake news stories going around, undermining the truth reported by establishment media. Here to answer our questions about how we can stop people from believing ridiculous notions, like Jeffrey Epstein not killing himself, is Spooky McSpookface. He's an expert in propaganda with the CIA. *Other* people's propaganda. Spooky, it's great to have you back on again. If you could just start out, why is it that you think people's faith in establishment media has never been lower?

Spooky: Well, incredibly racist people, egged on by the genetically-inclined-to-crime Russians, have been spreading information unapproved by the agencies, that can be very damaging.

MSNBC Host: Can you give us an example?

Spooky: Yes. Some people on social media are suggesting the U.S. should pull troops out of Afghanistan.

MSNBC Host: Shocking!

Spooky: I know. But this is only the tip of the iceberg. Some people are even suggesting we return Syrian oil fields to the Syrians.

MSNBC: Barbarians! Do these people have any idea how dangerous to world peace that would be?

Spooky: They have no idea. This is why people need someone to do their thinking for them. Why, it gets even worse than that. Some people are actually claiming that intelligence agencies are themselves spreading untruthful narratives.

MSNBC Host: Racists!

Spooky: You know, there are many people of color who work for the intelligence agencies, and when I hear such accusations, it makes me think Jim Crow has never really gone away.

MSNBC Host: I'm sorry but we're going to have to leave it there. We have just received breaking news. Unnamed intelligence officials have confirmed that Russia has done further unspecified bad stuff. Stay tuned for Rachel Maddow, who will undoubtedly speculate about what sort of bad stuff they may have done.

Rachel Maddow: Tonight...we have learned that Russia did bad stuff. Does Putin never sleep? I wonder. You know...Ted Cruz left the country lately, supposedlytogoonvacationwithhisfamily. But...it's a little odd...don't you think? I mean...leaving the country when a deadly Siberian storm was bearing down on his home state of Texas was not very good timing on his part. What if, and as of yet this has not been confirmed, what if he was making pee videos with Russian prostitutes? What if —

(Click)

Escaping The Matrix Part 1: The Media

We can never begin to grasp the truth, can never start to shape the world that needs to be, until we are willing to see beyond and reject the illusion our media has fabricated. We have to come to the understanding that they are not our friend, and that they do not have our best interests at heart. It is not their job to educate or enlighten us but to propagandize, distract, and divide us. The primary concern of the media is not human beings but profit. They do not speak a human language but a corporate one, because that is who they are and what they serve.

The media is in the hands of a very wealthy few. Their interests are to increase profit, decrease cost, and make a system that works for the very wealthy appear to be the best of all possible systems. Everything else is secondary. Commitment to truth is secondary. Creating an educated and informed citizenry is secondary.

Covering the most pressing issues of our day is secondary. Time and again it can be shown that the media covers issues that are not important but focuses instead on what is salacious and divisive. To them, Donald Trump was a Godsend.

The best thing the media can hope for is a sex scandal. Wars are nice but they have to do more work and be a little more aggressive in shaping the narrative. A good sex scandal has all the benefits of a war with none of the risk. Get a good sex scandal up and running and it will provide sufficient cover for the warmongers to bomb people overseas without the populace even noticing. Put some bimbo's boobs on the screen next to a picture of a married politician and nobody's going to care that children are being blown up by drone strikes.

As Russell Brand said, the people on the other side of the screens are not your friends. They seek to mold your opinions, want you to buy into the idea that money. rather than human beings, is what matters. Sure, there are many real human beings working to provide content, but as long as they are in the service of corporations for a paycheck, they are really no different than those who worked within the Nazi system: both subjugate their own humanity and connection to their fellow humans in order to further themselves in inhuman structures.

The media does not want you to feel powerful. They want you to subject yourselves to the authorities they promote. Their spokespeople, be it Rachel Maddow or Rush Limbaugh, are millionaires working for billionaires. They are paid obscene amounts of money to spread the opinions of the wealthy to the average American.

They want you to feel helpless so that you do not act to change things. They want you to feel helpless so that you are ready to accept the answers THEY provide, which you settle for even though you know deep down it is not what you need. They want you to feel stupid, so that you do not question authority.

And as the news outlets of the oligarchs preach to you the gospel of the sociopathically rich, so does the media attack you with their entertainment and advertisement arms. They have convinced you that their programming is therapeutic as an escape from a stressful and unpleasant reality. The truth is that daytime talk shows and nighttime drama have the potential to create an understanding in their audience that would lead to making reality less stressful and unpleasant. The truth CAN set you free but the media is more concerned with ensnaring you in endless unreality (the ultimate unreality being what they call reality TV).

This is why the media will not show you pictures of homeless people freezing to death in the cold but instead shows you people drinking beer on the beach.

Billionaires, and those who seek to advance themselves by spreading the gospel of billionaires, have no interest in providing you with the kind of morals and context you would need to make the world a better place. The very fact that they have billions of dollars proves where their values lie. They do not wish to make you smart but instead want to keep you ignorant. Why would it be otherwise? Why would people whose primary goal is to extract from others whatever they can, do something that would endanger their self-interest?

No, The Revolution Will Not Be Televised. The media exists to block the way. The media exists to place every available impediment and distraction between you and human progress, and its reach is quite pervasive. If we ever hope to get beyond our feelings of powerlessness, confusion, hopelessness, and division, we will have to see the corporate propaganda machine for what it is: a servant of the few and an enemy of the many.

The Media Will Never Back A Candidate You Would Want To Vote For

(Originally shared on 3-17-19 on Medium)

Here is the dilemma we now face: Any presidential candidate worth voting for will not get the media support needed to get elected, and any candidate the media is willing to support is not worth our votes. Oligarchy, the military industrial complex, and unaccountable intelligence agencies are the problem. And a media owned by the oligarchs, infiltrated by and in bed with intelligence agencies, and entirely subservient to the military industrial complex, is not about to let a candidate interested in serving the common citizen become president. It is the media's job, its raison d'être, to support war, wealth, and non-democratic means of government.

The media's the most powerful entity on earth. They have the power to make the innocent guilty and to make the guilty innocent, and that's power. Because they control the minds of the masses. — Malcolm X

It is media's job to prevent a challenge to arms manufacturers and pointless wars. You have never nor will you ever see a commercial news outlet come out against military intervention against another country. Nor will you ever hear anyone in the media say that military spending needs to be cut. It will never happen. Come out against war and you will lose your platform, as happened with Phil Donahue and Jessie Ventura when they opposed the Iraq War. Support war and you can spout outright lies and never fear losing a place in the media. Witness Brian Williams being given the opportunity to wax poetic about missiles after falsely recounting a story.

"The press of the United States? It is a parasitic growth that battens on the capitalist class. Its function is to serve the established by moulding public opinion, and right well it serves it." — Jack London, The Iron Heel

It is the media's job to prevent a challenge to oligarchy and the ultra-rich. You will not hear anyone attack oligarchs or the concentration of wealth into the hands of a few. Should anyone do so, the wrath of the media will soon fall upon them, as can be witnessed in the sudden attacks on Tucker Carlson after he spoke out against Jeff Bezos (He also spoke out against war in Syria, so that could play a factor, as well). Now, the pushback on Tucker Carlson may be perfectly legitimate, but it is odd that it was not so full-throated until this point, when a lot of what he has said has been around for a decade or so.

This is why oligarchs buy the news outlets, in order to shape the narrative in a way that paints them in a good light. This is why the richest man in the world, Jeff Bezos, bought the Washington Times. It wasn't because it would significantly add to his wealth, and it was not — as the media described it — an act of charity in order to help a struggling but necessary institution. Just reflect upon that notion for a little bit in order to savor the ridiculousness of what the media is trying to sell you.

"The Revolution Will Not Be Televised" — Gil Scott Heron

It is the job of the media to prevent a challenge to the unaccountable intelligence agencies. Ask yourself when was the last time you heard the media be skeptical of the CIA, FBI, NSA, etc. When was the last time there was a scandal regarding an intelligence agency where the media wasn't defending them? From Valerie Plame to James Comey to Robert Mueller, the spooks are always the good guys in any news story. Increasingly, they are portrayed as the good guys in Hollywood movies, as Black Panther demonstrates (It has come to this, the ludicrous idea that U.S.

intelligence agencies are friends to people of color around the world).

So let me reinterpret for you the mainstream media's primary assertion for why you shouldn't vote for candidates they do not approve. When they say "your candidate in unelectable", what they are really saying is "We will never give your candidate sufficient coverage to allow the majority of Americans to vote for him/her. Should the candidate you like (but they do not) get any kind of momentum, we (the media) will do everything in our power to undermine and smear him/her." This is the problem we will have to surmount if we are ever to use our democracy as an effective means of change.

Fortunately, the curtain that the media places over reality has never been shabbier. The greater the disparity between the reality and the narrative, the more they will have to stretch that curtain, and the more reality will peek through. We are observing it in many different ways, but until the curtain is pulled back or we no longer accept the picture drawn upon it, things will not make sense for us. That is why Donald Trump's success in 2016 was so shocking to so many: because it was so completely antithetical to the picture that had been painted by the media. It was outside the narrative, not in the script. But this was precisely why Trump had the success he had, (it wasn't because of a few Facebook ads). He chose to confront the media directly. He chose not to play their games. Most importantly, he did not bow down to the narrative the media insists all who receive air time must bow down to.

Until we have a prominent voice on the left who is willing to reject the corporate media's narrative, until there is a candidate too popular to ignore who will refuse to concede the talking points of the media, we are all playing the media's game, and all of politics will be serving the interests of those who control and own the media. Instead of a clown who performs in front of the curtain, we must have a candidate of integrity willing to pull back the curtain and let reality shine through. We can hasten the day this happens by individually rejecting the authority of a corporate media that time and again lies us into wars and tax cuts and trade deals that do not benefit the people but only enrich the financial interests of the few.

Addendum

The inspiration for this essay was watching Tulsi Gabbard on Steven Colbert. If you have any doubt that the media is willing to take down any candidate who speaks out against the war machine, please watch the Tulsi Gabbard interview. Rather than the typical piece he usually engages in, one of banal pleasantries and sycophantic softball questions, Colbert echoes the exact same talking points media "journalists" and talk show hosts have used every time Gabbard is given air time. It is an entirely humorless interview, save one lame attempt at the very end. As means of comparison, check out Colbert's interviews with Beto Rourke, Kamala Harris, and Hillary Clinton. There is a consistent lightheartedness in these other videos that is utterly lacking in the Tulsi Gabbard interview. Sadly, for a long time I thought of Steven Colbert as one of the leading lights of the Left.

A Conversation With The Media About Trump

This is a conversation I've been having with the media for the last 40 years. See if it makes sense to you:

<u>1989</u>

Media: This is Donald Trump, isn't he great?
Me: What makes him great?
Media: He's rich! That makes him the embodiment of all that is great about America.
Me: How does being rich make him great?
Media: Being rich means you are smart and hard-working. The fact that you do not already know this and aren't rich means that you are stupid. And lazy.
Me: I'll tell you what: you get Donald Trump to hold onto the back of a garbage truck and throw garbage all day with me and we'll see who's the harder worker. Or we can dig ditches. I've got the muscles and callouses to show I work hard. I can't tell how flabby this Trump guy is under that expensive suit.
Media: You're just jealous because he's smart and hardworking and has immense wealth.

Me: I just want to know he's thrown his share of garbage in life and dug his share of ditches. Does he really owe his wealth to hard work and brains or did he inherit it?

Media: Not only is he smart and hardworking, he's not afraid to take chances.

Me: That sounds rather reckless on his part. If there's anything I've been taught operating heavy machinery is that you need to minimize risk. I know people who've broken legs and had body parts ripped off taking chances on the job. When you take reckless chances, you risk not only your own well-being but the safety of others, as well. Play it safe and you never make a mess so big others need to clean it up for you. Like the time that guy got his push blade stuck in the truck by overpacking it and the rest of us had to dig out the garbage by hand.

Media: Oh dear, Donald Trump has had to declare bankruptcy.

Me: What did I tell you about taking big risks and ending up making a mess other people have to clean up?

Media: No, it's a good thing.

Me: Huh?

Media: That means Donald Trump has a chance to start over so he can show everyone how smart and hardworking he is.

Me: Why does he get a second chance? My friend who lost his arm in the power takeoff of a truck doesn't get his arm back. My roofer friend who fell off a roof doesn't get his mobility back. My friend who stuck his hand in a machine trying to save the company a few bucks doesn't get his fingers back.

Media: That's because they weren't smart and hardworking and daring like Donald Trump is. He wasn't afraid to take chances. Society needs to reward people like him.
Me: Whatever...

2004

Media: Are you watching Donald Trump's new reality show where he has a bunch of workers battle it out to see who will get to be hired by him?
Me: No, why should I?
Media: It's fun because he makes people grovel and lick his shoes and whoever grovels the least and licks his shoes less convincingly, he tells them they're fired.
Me: That sounds terrible. I'm glad I belong to a union so I don't have to kiss anybody's ass like that.
Media: Oh, that's just the way things need to be if society is going to be productive and America is going to succeed.
Me: I've found I've always been most productive when I'm able to work with others as equals in order to get a job done. I don't see how cruelty makes a business run any better.
Media: That's because you are stupid and lazy. If you were ambitious and intelligent, you would be licking Donald Trump's shoes in order to succeed, too.
Me: Whatever...

February, 2016

Media: Look at this!

Me: What am I looking at?

Media: It's Donald Trump's empty podium! He'll be standing here in a few minutes. Isn't it newsworthy?

Me: Are you out of your minds? You've been telling me I've been stupid and lazy for decades now, but at least I do my job and I do it well. You show me an empty podium and think you're doing your job well?

Media: Oh, we're not here to inform you, we're here to amuse you. And there is nothing quite as amusing as Donald Trump getting up on a stage and behaving like a buffoon, is there?

Me: I guess part of me is amused—the part of me that hates life. But I've been telling you for decades there is nothing of value to be found in this man. Why do you keep making him out to be Dudley Goddamn Do Right?

Media: Because he is entertaining. And when he entertains you, it means more money for us. And the magic of the market dictates that when we make money, EVERYBODY benefits.

Me: Whatever...

February 2017

Media: This is something stupid Donald Trump said, taken out of context so it makes him look even more stupid. Isn't it horrible?

Me: What?

Media: Donald Trump is an evil Nazi traitor to the country.

Me: Isn't this the man who you've been holding up as the role model for our entire country for decades now.

Media: We will not respond to that assertion. Donald Trump is the most evil person who has ever existed.

Me: Look, I'm no fan of Donald Trump. And I definitely don't think he should be our president, but the people—influenced as they have been by the media for decades—have spoken, and-

Media: Putin has spoken, more like it.

Me: What?

Media: There is only one possible explanation why people voted for Trump—Russian interference.

Me: Oh, dear sweet Jesus. Why can't you own up to your own guilt in getting him elect—

Media: Vladimir Putin, using memes, Pokemon Go, Porpoises with cameras, and Jill Stein, is working to undermine not only the integrity of our election but the reputation of the media.

Me: Whatever...

<u>2028</u>

Media: Did you see Donald Trump give a piece of candy to Michelle Obama and dance with Ellen Degeneres? Isn't he wonderful?

Me: Whatever...

Another Conversation With The Media (And Politicians)

Media And Politicians: We support peace and democracy.

Me: Well I'm glad to hear that.

M&P: Which is why we need to confront the evil dictator of Nation X.

Me: Confrontation sounds very much like war, which is the opposite of peace.

M&P: We need to remove the evil dictator of Nation X in order to restore democracy, which will bring about peace and prosperity.

Me: Wasn't the president —

M&P: Evil dictator.

Me: All right. Wasn't the evil dictator of Nation X democratically elected? I fail to see how overthrowing a democratically elected presi — I mean dictator, is in any way democratic.

M&P: The evil Dictator of Nation X was not elected by a real democratic process the way our benevolent leaders in the United States and those in nations we are allied to, such as Israel and Saudi Arabia, were.

Me: Wait, what? Saudi Arabia's leaders are democratically elected?

M&P: Never mind that. The evil dictator of Nation X-

Me: Look, it's getting hard to keep typing "the evil dictator of Nation X" all the time. Do you mind if we just use an acronym, maybe something like Ted Onx?

M&P: Actually, we use that same acronym in our template for how to overthrow governments that are not supporting our interests and the economic interests of oil companies. Oops. I mean, yes, let's call him Ted Onx.

Me: Good. Now, I understand that Ted Onx is probably not a real great guy, but don't you think that by using war and non-democratic means that we are behaving in the same manner you accuse Ted Onx of?

M&P: We despise violence and support democracy, but in this unique circumstance there is no other option than dropping bombs in order to protect the sacred values of democracy.

Me: Hey, wait a minute, isn't that what you said about the evil dictator of Nation W?

M&P: That was a mistake.

Me: Oh, okay. Hey, wait a minute. Didn't you say it was a mistake when you used violence to overthrow the evil dictator of Nation V?

M&P: Yes we did. And if you'll notice, after we overthrew the government of Nation V, reduced the country to a ravaged, anti-democratic smoldering crater, we apologized for being too credulous for believing the unsubstantiated assertions of those who led us into that war. So you see, we're all good.

Me: I remember that now. Didn't you promise to do a better job of digging for the truth the next time?

M&P: Most assuredly, because we are trustworthy sources of information who only want to provide you with the truth.

Me: So you got rid of all the journalists who uncritically supported the lies and promoted and rewarded all the journalists who got the story right?

M&P: We are not judgmental. Sometimes journalists get a story wrong, but they're trying really hard to get it right this time.

Me: But they're behaving in the exact same fashion as they did when they uncritically supported the last war against Nation W. And Nation V. And Nation U. And-

M&P: We don't engage in whataboutisms. Besides, this situation is unique. Babies are being ripped from incubators and used to manufacture weapons of mass destruction.

Me: That sounds a little far-fetched.

M&P: And you, sir, sound like a Ted Onx apologist.

Me: Well, could you at least tell me what the journalists and politicians who got the stories of Nation V and nation W might think?

M&P: We would love to, but we're afraid they no longer work for us. Many of them are now at RT, and we can't recommend you go there, because RT is a government-supported propaganda outlet.

Me: And what would you call a media conglomerate that time after time echoes the unsubstantiated claims of its government in order to lead us into war?

M&P: Boy, have you seen what the evil dictator of Nation Y is doing? We really need to do something about him.

The Indie Revolution

Though it may sound somewhat paradoxical, "Indies of the world unite!"

It occurred to me recently just how much I have dropped out of mainstream society. The music I listen to is of the independent variety, bands you have never heard of and yet ones that are capable of producing brilliant music without the assistance of the corporate machinery. The authors I know are indie authors, the news I consume comes from non-establishment sources, the movies I watch are increasingly indie films. I have joined a food co-op in order to support local farmers, and try to buy as much as possible from local and small businesses. I try to avoid chain restaurants and support the mom and pop eateries. I am trying really hard to build an indie career.

In short, I have become an indie. The corporate world has little appeal to me anymore. When I was younger I wanted nothing more than a Quarter Pounder and Fries, was content with viewing whatever sequel was playing at the multiplex. I walked down the path of least resistance and didn't contemplate much where it was leading me.

But in the back of my mind, the pit of my stomach, or perhaps in the depths of my soul, there was a voice telling me that the path of least resistance was not leading to a very healthy place. As I learned and grew, I began to realize that McDonald's cheeseburgers were not very good for me, the environment, the local community, or the animals that gave their lives to increase my calorie count. But for years, even after realizing it was not the best thing to do, I couldn't seem to keep away. Even today I am not completely safe from the occasional Big Mac attack.

McDonald's is no different than any powerful corporate entity. They appeal to the weaker aspects of our humanity, lull our adult capacities to sleep while preying upon our more childish desires and fears. Corporations are like that, because they don't really care about people at all, but only profits. If they do profess to care about people it is only so that they may increase profits. Corporations are means by which normal human moral concerns are stripped away in order to reduce human interactions into economic transactions. If you belong to a corporation and suggest that moral considerations be placed above economic ones, you will be punished for it.

So, being a human being, I have rejected the corporate mentality that says everything can be reduced down to financial transactions that are to the benefit of corporations. That the only goal in life is to be of worth to the corporation and the corporate society so that you will be richly rewarded for your strengthening of it. I am attempting to reclaim my humanity from the corporate paradigm just as our forefathers sought to reclaim their humanity from the influence of their rulers across the ocean. And like our founding fathers, we will need to work together in order to accomplish our independence. We must define ourselves as a group so that the corporate media must recognize and react to us rather than ignore us and our argument.

The line that divides the two narratives — the indies and the corporatists — is quite evident, though corporate media, propaganda, and marketing have done all in their power to blur and obscure that line. On one side of the line is art for art's sake, on the other, art for profit's sake. On one side is food for humans, the other, profit and dominance for Monsanto and Archer Daniels Midland. On one side is...well, you get the idea.

I am well aware that corporations deliver necessary goods and services to people, and that I myself am far from being independent of them. I type these words on a Hewlett Packard laptop using Microsoft Word, use AT&T, Facebook, and other corporations as means to share this message with others. Corporations are necessary to us in so many ways, at least in the world as it now is.

But they have become the master rather than the servant to humanity. Let not their necessity convince us that we are hypocrites for suggesting they have become too powerful. This situation must be dealt with, human beings must find within themselves the desire and the power to reclaim their own destiny from corporate entities and the corporate mentality. Corporate-produced material goods, food, and media, are not always possible to avoid, but we need to become conscious of our relationship with them and reduce our dependence as much as possible. We need to go about the business of creating an environment that puts human rights and interests above corporate ones. And that is what I refer to as an indie revolution.

We need to, as much as possible, become independent of the corporate entities that seek to own us as they own any other commodity. The very notion of "indie" is a call for independence, for freedom, for autonomy. Go see a local musician perform live. Buy local art. Read the writing of indie authors and journalists. Buy from local farmers and shop at local stores. Once you begin looking at life through an indie lens you will see all the decisions you can make and the power you have to alter the world in which we live.

The line that is blurred must be made clear. The corporate media must react to the reality of the indie revolution. We must define the terms, and not allow the corporate media to shape the debate. We must not react but instead demand *they* react to what real live human beings in the pursuit of human values see as the way forward to a better world.

To this end, it must be made clear that corporate media is no longer the voice of authority, That their very corporate values disqualify them from being allowed to shape our view of the world, because the only view of the world they can give us is a corporate one. Let the line be drawn quite clearly and always remind corporate interests that they are not on humanity's side of it.

To this end, we must view corporate politicians as nothing more than employees of a corporate system that places profit above human well-being and the very planet that allows for our existence. I will not tell you never to vote for a corporate politician, though I personally find it foolish, but if you do so without making it clear that you and not they are the master in the relationship, you have given away everything that is important to you for the promises of liars.

To this end we must embrace an indie lifestyle and build an indie movement that places human values and human perspectives above corporate profit and growth. If corporations say they wish to serve us, then let them serve us, but no longer should we allow them to be our masters.

The Media's War On Spirituality

Spirituality is either the result of having a comfortable enough place to reflect upon the meaning and purpose of human existence, or else it is the result of such suffering that one has no choice but to retreat inward in search of ways to cope. The most spiritual among us are those who embrace both ends of the spectrum, those who forsake physical comforts in order to have the time to focus on the meaning that can be found in simplicity. I refer to the religious, who can be found in any primitive society, from Buddhists to Taoists, to Christians, Muslims and Jews. I refer also to primitive societies because I wonder if it is even possible to retreat from the modern society that now exists.

Economically, we should have arrived at a point where we are all comfortable enough to afford the time and space necessary to reflect upon spiritual matters. But the economic engine that was so good at creating convenience and solutions to physical want also demands our undivided attention. A capitalist economy soon realized it needed to become a consumer society in order to further itself, so that wealth creation went from beyond the merely physical to the psychological. In order to maintain a system that can give happiness on merely a physical level, they needed to eradicate from people's consciousness any thoughts of achieving happiness through non-economic means.

When people are not actively purchasing or consuming or else creating goods or services for others, they must either be lulled into a stupor or else be driven to distraction by emotional provocation. They must be given constant distractions so that their thoughts never stray to the spiritual perspective, which revolts in the face of such mindless creation and consumption. To distract from the spiritual, they must never let minds stay too long on a single subject. A mind left alone too long might start out on a path of self-directed thoughts. Interrupt it every few minutes or even seconds, and the mind is forced to respond to outside stimuli and forget whatever internal ideas that might be bubbling beneath the surface. Scatter the pieces of the puzzle at regular intervals, and the puzzle solver will never be able to put them together to form a coherent image.

Thus we have commercials on television to take us from those very rare instances when a compelling argument or narrative is taking place. And what was once a break every fifteen minutes or so has become more frequent. Live shows, that once had a single camera resting upon a scene for moments at a time as it played out, have been replaced by the hyper-editing introduced to us on MTV in the 80s.

News channels not only give us one story, they give us many concurrently. They have the narrative spoken by the host, but they also have a running stream of information below it. Add to that the constantly shifting graphics all about and the mind is always in motion, never permitted to orient itself.

This is not a stylistic choice, not some mere fad that has come and will then make way for some other style. The immense amounts of information that is thrown at you on CNN and elsewhere is not an attempt to keep you as informed as possible in a hectic and changing world. It is a way to ensure your mind is always kept busy, because a busy mind is always concerned with the surface noise, and is never able to plunge the depths of issues. The media has created a kinetic Potemkin village, one of pure flash and no substance. It is not merely useless, it is distracting. No useful knowledge can be gained from such a system of information dispersal. It does not permit you to connect with your rational nor spiritual aspects, it merely demands you absorb. It does not give, it demands obeisance.

The media is not there to inform you. It is not there to help you become a more active member of a democratic society. It is there to keep your emotions heightened so your intellect is never in the driver's seat. It is there to prime you for the people who make the commercials and pay the bills. It is there to wear down your defenses. And since it is so all-encompassing, it inevitably will. When it does not leave you feeling stupid it will leave you feeling helpless. For those most in its control, you will be left feeling intelligent and powerful while having a grasp neither on truth nor on the reins of power.

But as powerful and omnipresent as the media is, it needs your help. It requires you to betray your most basic values in order for it to be effective. If you stay true to the values your parents and your teachers and your religious institutions have sought to instill in you, the media cannot control you. It may dress itself up as your mother, but it will never tell you to share with others. It may say it speaks for Christ, but it will never tell you to cast your bread upon the waters. It may quote from revered historical figures, but it will do so only in order to corrupt the spirit of what they have said. Peace and love are perhaps the most revered words echoed by family and church, but they will never be spoken in the media, because peace and love don't help sell automobiles. The degree to which you do not hear the Sermon On The Mount spoken on your television is the degree to which the media is working against your best interests and the interests of all humanity.

What can you do to escape from the insidious influence of the media? Find a source untainted by it. Pick up an old book, watch an old (black and white) movie. Step outside your era because it is only in this way you can step outside of the cultural milieu created by a media that has become both incredibly concentrated and far-reaching. If you must consume current media, then listen to genuinely independent news, art, and music. Get outside and in touch with the physical world around you, with whatever nature is left to you. Dig in the garden, walk in the woods, listen to the birds. Rebuild the connections that were all your forefathers ever knew so that you have a frame of reference built on something of substance.

It is time to step away from the television and get out in the streets. It is time to stop listening to the lies and start speaking the truth. Because here is the idea most feared by a mechanized and monetized media, the secret it seeks above all else to keep from you: that you are in control not only of your own life but are part of a society that can direct the future for itself, without the need for them. We as rational and caring human beings can construct a world where lying and coercion will be unnecessary, where force will be seen as a tool of the unjust. Because in order to build a functional society, you don't need to be controlled, you need to be liberated.

TV's Children

Does capitalism have your children's best interests at heart? Do you ever feel the need to protect them from what is shown on corporate-owned television, to restrict their young eyes not only from the programming itself but from the commercials?

Do you think the foods that are little more than sugar and processed flour are a result of anything other than the capitalist's desire to prey on the young and the helpless, or do you actually think it is the fault of parents that children are facing an epidemic of obesity and diabetes?

I watched another of those video clips the other day about college students who couldn't tell you who won the Civil War and yet could name who Brad Pitt was married to and what show Snookie was on. Like everyone else I was shockingly disappointed by the results and yet I shouldn't have been surprised.

You see, a lot of people in their disgust blame the youth of today. They blame the education system, the government, the liberals, etc. But what those people are missing is the fact that the youth know what society teaches them. They are not ignorant, they have learned what society has told them is important. And what society tells them is that Snookie and the love lives of celebrities are important.

After all, we could have a different system if we wanted to. We could have media that actually teaches us something worth knowing. We could have a history channel that has programming about history, an arts and entertainment channel that has actual art and artists on it, or a music channel that deals with music. We could have whatever kind of media we want; it is a free country, we should decide.

But that's not what we have. We are constantly being told that we live in the society we wanted, that our society is the result of our decisions. Yet the world is not what we want it to be. Why is that? Are we stupid? Assuredly we have our flaws, our weaknesses and are capable of being distracted by things not so important to us. Yes, we are imperfect, but that is not the whole story.

The fact is, our weaknesses are being played upon. There are those who work very hard and are paid very well to make sure we don't focus on what is best for us but instead become distracted by that which is not vital to us. They are artists when it comes to playing upon our baser instincts, our sexual urges, our insecurities, and a myriad of other shortcomings. They manipulate us—there is no other term for it—into becoming pliable consumers willing to buy what they are selling.

The blame for that lies squarely on the capitalists who own our media, who for the better part raise our children because they have taught us it is our duty to be at work rather than with them. We do our best to instill in them human values rather than corporate values but the television, the radio, and now a host of other media have far more of their time and attention than we ever will. We can try to keep them in a bubble, and some of us do, but they will not be able to avoid those others of their generation, the majority, that have been raised with values that are alien to the human race. Corporate values.

They cleverly tie cute cartoon creatures with sugary treats, designer labels, and violence. They hyper-sexualize adolescence and brand them when they are young so that by the time they are adults, they will not even see the cage that has built for them.

Aldous Huxley saw it clearly enough in 1931, and put it all down for us to read in Brave New World. He saw the manipulation of young minds so that the adults they grew into would be incapable of thinking outside of established parameters. You can bet that advertisers envisioned it too. Of course they did not see the damage it would cause. Their narrow vision only saw the profit they could make from such a system. They pursued it the way any unthinking creature in an excited state pursues its prey. And they were very good at what they did.

So the next time you see people knowing nothing about their history and everything about the Kardashians, let it be known that our education system, the real one, the one that is fully funded, is doing its job capably.

My Parents Taught Me Not To Waste. Television, Not So Much.

Recently, my wife and I noticed our kitchen garbage was smelling pretty bad and needed to be taken out. So straight away we looked around the house for any trash in the waste paper baskets we could fill up the bag with. After that we went through the fridge to clear out any old food containers. It was only once we had a full garbage bag that it occurred to us: we could have just taken out a mostly empty bag.

But it hadn't occurred to us. That's not how we were raised. A garbage bag had to be crammed full before you took it outside. It was just...the way.

A while before that happened, I found myself doing something I realized my parents would be proud of me for. I wasn't accomplishing anything that would bring renown to the family name. What I was doing was making a peanut butter sandwich. But the part I felt they would approve of was that I was using a spatula to get the last bits of peanut butter out of the jar. Because that's what they taught me to do when I was young, though it was something I at that time resisted. Because it made extra work for me. But that was the reality they grew up in, both of them being raised during The Great Depression when waste was not an option.

Thrift was an inconvenient idea for people of my generation. We had so much in the way of material possessions and cheap goods it really was easier for us to throw something away and just get a new one. We were a generation torn between an older way of doing things and a new one.

I don't know about people younger than myself, but anyone my age or older experienced it: that moment when you brought an appliance or an electronic device to a repair shop to have it fixed, only to be told that it would be cheaper to buy a new one than repair it. We all felt the wrongness of it. In the end, though, we were all taught to save a buck wherever possible. But we knew, we knew, that it shouldn't be this way. We knew we were participating in a system that didn't make sense. And yet we trusted the system, trusted progress, trusted authority…we trusted something. Because up until then it made sense to trust. The system was working, and it seemed like we were progressing, and those telling us to trust didn't seem all that scary.

But that trust we had in a system has led us to where we are today. We live in a society where half the food we grow is wasted while the great lakes are being turned into dead zones due to the intensive fertilizer used to grow food we don't even eat. We live in a society where people rent storage units to hold the possessions they don't have room for. And the real cost for all the waste we engage in is finally becoming unavoidable.

If I could tell one thing to young people today it would be what my parents told me. It was the same thing their parents told them and so on, back into prehistory. Do not take what you do not need, do not take seconds until you are sure everyone else got a first serving. If you put something on your plate, you eat it.

Do not waste because there are others in the world who do not have enough. Do not throw things away that are still good just because you want something better. The Baby Boomer generation hated the "There are kids starving in China" line, but that is only because the television spent more time raising them than their parents. An entire generation was hijacked by Madison Avenue to go against everything every adult ever tried to instill into their young.

We have had it drilled into our heads that individual decisions and actions do not matter, but they do. They matter because values matter. This was never in contention until radio and television and the internet ushered in a new value system that served advertisers. It was a value system that was in direct opposition to what every parent tried to instill into their children until the time when advertisers had more influence on children than their own parents. That shift happened around the time when I was a child and television had established its place in American households. Let us be clear that what was established was an usurpation by corporate values over human values. It is the difficult but necessary task of each of us to overturn the values coup and reassert human values once more.

The values we live by in our everyday lives have a ripple effect. They change not only the way we live our individual lives but also the way we perceive how society should be run. We need to live our values in order for them to be translated into society at large. The big changes society needs, which we know it needs, will not come about of their own accord. They will not come about when the right people are elected or the right technology becomes available. It sure won't come about through the media. It will come about when people live out simple but timeless values.

It's time to take the stinky garbage bag of corporate values to the curb.

The News Is What's Newsworthy

Once again, I was made aware of a current event and dove into a provided article in order to learn the facts about it. I'm not sure what the source was, I think it was something like The Daily Beast or Buzz Feed or the Cranky Turtle, or something like that. I miss the days when news agencies didn't try to have hipster sounding names and stuck to names like The Post, The Tribune, or The Reporter. At least then you knew they were owned by establishment types, whereas now you're led to believe they are led by hip young counter-culture types.

The news of the day was that Disney fired Gina Carano for making controversial remarks on social media. I clicked on the link to read the actual article to find out what she said. I don't think people are actually expected to do this, I think they are supposed to take their cues from headlines and have their opinions provided to them rather than making up their own minds. Nevertheless, the purveyors of news feel like they have to give the appearance of actual reporting by including an article to go along with the headline. It's a time-waster for suckers like me who hope to find actual substance in it.

It turns out that the headline these days is the frosting on a sponge cake. And it's made from an actual sponge. There is no actual "there" there, anymore, not in mainstream media. My experience with corporate journalism articles since Trump became president has been this: Enticing headline which makes me want to know more, followed by paragraphs that reassert the headline without giving actual evidence for the assertion, peppered with links that don't provide the actual evidence I'm looking for, often ending in an admission that the actual assertions might not be true. Look at any Russiagate article you've shared with others with a critical eye and you'll understand what I'm talking about.

Before going any further, I would like to point out that I am not and have never been a Republican or a conservative. I have always considered myself to be firmly on the left, which is why I've always been sensitive regarding the idea that people's livelihoods can be ruined because of the way they exercise their freedom of speech. I always thought this was a liberal idea. After all, Joe McCarthy was a Republican who smeared and ruined the lives of many a leftist. But it is also worth noting that it was during a Democratic administration that the silencing of Paul Robeson took place. It was under a Democratic administration that Eartha Kitt's career was derailed after she spoke out against the Vietnam War in front of Ladybird Johnston.

There is one article on the firing of Gina Carano that serves as a template for what is wrong with journalism in general. Please keep in mind the title says

Here's Why Gina Carano Was Fired From 'The Mandalorian', the key word being "Why".

According to the article, "she reshared a post that seemed to suggest having a differing political view in 2021 was similar to being Jewish during the Holocaust". A statement from Lucasfilm states "Her social media posts denigrating people based on their cultural and religious identities are abhorrent and unacceptable."

That's a big stretch there. Taken on faith that Carano's intent was to suggest having a differing political view was similar to being Jewish during the Holocaust, it does not equate to "denigrating people based on their cultural and religious identities" In fact, it implies that Carano is identifying with the Jews, not denigrating them. Nor is the post intended to equate Republicans with Jews so much as it is to equate the current political climate with something capable of becoming comparable to Nazi Germany. Her crime is one of hyperbole and a demonstration of Godwin's Law, but I do not see it as a denigration of people based on their cultural and religious identities.

The comparison of one's political opponents to Nazis is overused, but there is some value to it. You don't want to wait until eugenics is in full swing to start comparing people to Nazis. It's the kind of thing you want to nip in the bud, so in my opinion, it is safer to compare bad behavior to Nazism than it is to worry about hurting people's sensibilities.

Besides, it's not like Democrats have not been engaging in the exact same behavior for four years. Type in an image search for "Trumpler" and see what you come up with (Let me know how many pages of images you find).

So is that the trespass she is accused of? Comparing the current political climate to Nazi Germany? I guess the way to prove her wrong would be to incite a mob on social media to demand she be fired from her job, right?

There's more, though, than just that one tweet, I get it. There was a string of unpopular things she shared on social media, this was merely the final straw. Apparently, she shared memes that "made fun of the mask mandate in California, compared former President Donald Trump's second impeachment trial to Groundhog Day, and claimed Jeffrey Epstein didn't kill himself."

In terms of spreading the belief that Jeffrey Epstein didn't kill himself, few people believe the official story. I know exactly one person who implied he did. Virtually everybody knows there's more to the story than we are being told, and many just shorthand the assertion that the media is lying by saying "Epstein didn't kill himself." Do I personally think he did? How would I know, the cameras that were supposed to be watching him didn't work. But everybody knows that it's fishy as hell. Even the media people whose job it is to silence discussion on Jeffrey Epstein know it, even if they can't say it.

As for her comparing Trump's second impeachment to Groundhog Day, is this seriously a reason for getting someone fired? Seriously?

Finally, there is the issue of her making fun of California's mask mandate. On this issue I personally disagree with her, at least I think I do. I'm not personally familiar with California's mask mandate, and I'm not sure what exactly she said, though I suspect it would be nothing I would try to get someone fired for. Let us delve further into the article and get to the specifics.

Except that there *are* no further tweets or other social media shares to be found in the article. Let me correct myself, there are no further tweets found in the article by Gina Carana. Instead the article shares angry tweets by anonymous tweeters calling for Carana to be fired. Within one is the assertion that she has expressed transphobic sentiments. But the article does not go on to share any evidence to back up the claim of an anonymous person on Twitter. Let me be clear: this article includes the assertion of an anonymous person on Twitter, and then does absolutely nothing to say if that assertion is true or false.

And this passes for journalism. Maybe it's just me, but if I were paid to report on the reason why someone in the public eye lost her job for voicing her political opinions, I would do the work and provide the actual social media posts she made, rather than the angry tweets of anonymous people.

I was introduced to this story by someone sharing another article. It was an article that told me how I should perceive the situation without providing me with the evidence I needed to make up my own mind. I responded to the social media post by saying I could not find the actual statements she made or shared. Someone else commented that I should follow the links in the article. That person had assumed that actual paid journalists would provide such information.

But I had long ago discovered differently. There were links, yes, but nothing to anything that provided any evidence.

And there is nothing unusual about this. Pay attention to any controversial article you come across and see if the links provided are actually being used to provide evidence or merely included to make the appearance of providing evidence.

Journalism in our era is not there to provide you with information, it is there to provide you with opinion. But if you take exception to anything provided by establishment media, you are accused of not accepting the facts or reality. Arguing your case will never amount to anything.

They've got this down to a science. They have propaganda and manipulation of the masses down to a science. In the nearly one hundred years since the nephew of Sigmund Freud, Edward Bernays, began using psychological principles for marketing and propaganda purposes, think tanks and government entities have learned a lot. You have to be aware of how this stuff works if you don't want to fall prey to it. Read everything critically, with the knowledge that there is always someone trying to manipulate your feelings and how you view reality.

Again, I am not and have never been a member of the Republican Party. I am not writing what I am writing to defend them or Gina Carano or any particular position. I am writing this in the attempt to hold Democrats and the (alleged) left media to a standard that rises above FOX News or Alex Jones. Right now, I often wonder if they're even capable of rising to the same sad standard.

What A New York Times Editor Looks Like

The New York Times is arguably THE newspaper of note. "All the news that's fit to print" reads their motto. As a child I knew this to be a serious newspaper because it didn't have a comics section. As a young adult, I knew it to be an intelligent publication because their crossword puzzle was so much harder than any other paper's. From that time to now, I always had an image of those in charge of the newspaper, an unknown and unknowable group of intellectuals who came from the very best schools and worked their way up the ranks to at last sit at the peak of the journalistic mountain. Journalistic gods who could not be questioned but only admired.

When I imagined an editor at the Gray Lady, I pictured...well, a gray lady. Or a gray man. Someone seasoned by a career in journalism. Someone who had seen it all, who had travelled throughout the world and gotten to know the most influential and interesting people on the planet. Someone who had sat in trenches with soldiers in wartime and been witness to the suffering of ordinary people as the great events of our age played out. Then I watched Bari Weiss, opinions page editor for The New York Times, on Joe Rogan's podcast. Not at all what I had imagined. Below is a link to the interview if you care to follow along:

https://www.youtube.com/watch?v=xpurFfcSNfU&t=190s

The very first words out of her mouth set the tone: "Oh, I don't know. I don't know who can beat him (Donald Trump)". It is a window into her soul. Clearly it is the horse race that is of primary concern to her, not issues. Eleanor Roosevelt said "Great minds discuss ideas; average ones discuss events; small minds discuss people." Hers is obviously not a great mind, and it could be argued that it is not the event itself but the outsized personality of Trump that demands her attention.

Obvious too is her vested interest in the subject. She does not sit back as would be expected of an editor, apart from and above the fray, objective like any professional journalist should be. There is a clear bias in her viewpoint, which Joe Rogan cleverly feeds.

The next time she opens her mother to speak, it is to say: "Duh".

Her third utterance begins with a repeat of her first: "I don't know who can beat him right now. And I'm sc... I don't know." It's pretty apparent she was about to say "I'm scared", and then stopped, remembering that as a journalist she's not supposed to insert her own emotions and feelings into her writing or speech.

Keep in mind now we are discussing an editor of the opinions section for the most prestigious newspaper in the United States, not some gum-cracking secretary for The Enquirer. One would assume she has beaten out virtually every other person with a journalism degree in the country. Chris Hedges isn't even worthy of a job with the NYT.

Okay, now fast forward to one and a half minutes in, when Joe Rogan mentions Tulsi Gabbard as one of those running in the Democratic primary. There is an immediate reaction from Bari, and she utters the word "montras (mispronunciation of monstrous)". Clearly she has deeply felt opinions of why Tulsi is a bad candidate. Let's listen to her explain them.

"Monstrous...ideas."

"She's an Assad toady."

Joe Rogan: "What's that mean? What's a toady?"

At this point Bari is uncertain of her own argument, even though she is so obviously viscerally attached to it. She looks off-camera for confirmation.

Berri: "I think that I used that word right. Jamie, can you look up what toady means?"

So obviously it is not a word she uses often. Hence, the statement "she's an Assad toady" is not a position she came to on her own but rather she is parroting what she has heard another or others say. She then hammers home her unfamiliarity with the word she just used by misspelling it to Jamie: "t-o-a-d-i-e". Keep in mind she works in print journalism. At America's premier newspaper. As an editor.

Joe Rogan: "What does that mean?"

Berri: "I think it means what I think it means."

Whenever you see someone expressing thoughts in words they are not familiar with, it is because they are expressing thoughts they did not think themselves. To further the point that the argument she makes did not evolve from actual thoughts in her own mind, she answers Joe Rogan's question "So she's an Assad sycophant, is that what you're saying?"

Berri: "Yeah, that's pr-...that's known."

So obviously it's proven and known, but to whom? If it was proven and known to Berri, she would have facts or arguments to back up such an assertion, right? I mean, she is the editor of the opinions page of The New York Times. Who on this planet should be more qualified to back up a statement with a compelling and fact-packed argument? But that is not the case, so it's simply that she has her opinion on good authority. In other words, she as a journalist and editorial writer and editor, is doing nothing more than parroting the opinions of others, the very opposite of what one should expect from someone in her position. She is not a free thinker providing perspective and facts to other free thinkers, she is part of a chain of command that funnels down the official position from her bosses to her readers. I'm guessing there have been no opinion pieces in the New York Times about Tulsi Gabbard that does not call her a toady or at least imply it.

I do not accuse her of being a censor. She's just not that bright or self-aware. It is clear from the interview she thinks she's a real journalist. She's assuredly received enough pats on the head and "good girls" from those above her to believe what she's doing is quality work in the same vein as Edward R. Murrow, Molly Ivins, or H. L. Mencken. But if she had the same desire to dig for and share the truth as them, she would not be where she is now.

Bari Weiss has very strong opinions without any idea of why she has them. One would be tempted to say she was unfit to run a high school newspaper but she is precisely the kind to be chosen: the kind who will never ever rock the boat or inconvenience power. She has proven herself time after time in a system that weeds out the trouble makers, the free thinkers, and the truth tellers. Hell, she doesn't even seem capable of standing on equal footing while talking politics with a guy who had people eat bugs on Fear Factor and does commentary on cage fighting.

Take one more look. This is the best of the best, the crème de la crème corporate media has to offer. Now look at what indie journalism and indie commentators have to say, and tell me which impresses you more, which is more deserving of your time.

https://www.youtube.com/watch?v=jS-sxJFn6O0&t=876s

Spreading Gossip Ruins Lives, Especially When The Gossip Comes From The CIA

If you share a news article, it is your responsibility to research the veracity of the article, otherwise it is simply gossip. We might think gossip is harmless, but it ruins lives. And when it is gossip planted by intelligence agencies that exist to promote

U.S. dominance all over the world, it could quite possibly ruin hundreds of millions of lives.

Here's how a rumor starts: Some nefarious individual has an agenda and so whispers an idea into the ear of someone whose job it is to collect news. Now, collecting news, like picking apples, is hard work. So neither the apple picker nor the journalist are going to question too much when someone drops what they're working to get right onto their lap. But if you're a responsible fruit picker, you should give that apple a quick inspection to make sure it's not rotten.

But the paid gossip thinks even a rotten apple is a juicy item. The only thing different between a gossip and a journalist at this point is that a journalist makes sure to be precise about the unverifiable information they receive.

The nefarious rumor starter knows which ears to whisper into first. They only speak to the most respectable news institutions, usually The New York Times (NYT) and The Washington Post (WaPo). They do this to give their rumors a veneer of legitimacy. The NYT and WaPo, respected institutions that they are, will qualify the story they report by mentioning somewhere in the article that the entire story relies on anonymous sources within agencies whose job it is to create rumors to advance their agenda. Okay, they don't say it quite like that, but they do admit—if you read it carefully— that they have no actual proof for anything they've said in the article.

But that's just how a rumor is born, not how it spreads. Like some infectious disease in a country crammed with people who don't believe in masks, it gets around quickly. First the other news outlets take the story and run with it. Because, as I've said before, why pick fruit when ripe ones are already falling onto your lap? Because the second tier gossips can't stake claim to breaking the rumor...er, news, it is their job to put a twist to it. And in twisting it, the first thing they tend to do is drop the "according to unnamed sources working for agencies that exist to spread misinformation that+ supports their agendas" part of the story. You see, since they're reporting second hand, they can now claim they got their information from The New York Times rather than from those unsavory rumor mongers who have been known to tell a whopper or two in their time that have led to a few million people dying in needless wars.

Now it used to be when people got news, they paid for it. And having paid for a newspaper, they took the time to actually read it. That's not how news works in the 21st Century. Today people mostly receive their news for free, and since it is free and abundant, they have no appreciation for it and merely take it in on a superficial level. Today, people get their news from headlines.

Since nobody pays for their sources of information anymore, the providers of information have had to look for other sources of income. Which is to say that the sources of information are no longer working for you, they are working for others whose intent it is to get you to believe what they want you to believe. To that end, they are more concerned about grabbing your attention than educating you. They are more interested in providing cheap content than insightful articles. In short, our journalistic institutions have become click-bait farms. And gossip mongers, willing ears for those with stories to tell.

Once unsubstantiated rumors have been echoed through the establishment media in order to give it a perceived respectability, it is then bounced around social media by those who were told when they were young that gossip was just a sin but never really saw the harm in it. From that point, the damage has been done. Because no matter how unsubstantiated the gossip is, it makes a mess. It's like throwing a mudball at someone in a white dress, you're never going to get the stain out. Start a rumor, and it will always be in the consciousness of the public no matter how wrong it was. Like pee tapes. Or Weapons Of Mass Destruction.

Which is why your mother always told you, don't be a gossip. It hurts innocent people while those who started the gossip just sit back and smile.

Jeffrey Epstein And The Silence Of The Media

(Originally published November 13, 2019 on my blog James Rozoff, Solutionist)

Those who would bother to listen to my arguments in the midst of the Russiagate madness—there were a few—would ask me incredulously, "Do you think everybody in the media is lying?" I would reply that I had no way of knowing what was going on inside their heads or their motivations for falling in with the herd, but their behavior was not the sort that is exhibited by journalists behaving in a professional, skeptical manner. People couldn't understand how nearly every single news outlet could get a story wrong. I too was astounded by it, but just because I couldn't explain how such widespread hysteria was possible didn't mean it wasn't happening. When the news tells me it's snowing and I look outside to see it is a warm sunny day, I'm going to go with my own common sense. I'm surprised more people don't remember how they were sold the lie of WMDs or babies being tossed to the floor from incubators.

Flash forward to August of this year. A convicted pedophile with ties to incredibly important people in the United States and elsewhere is found dead in his jail cell. The most important criminal in a United States prison dies and the two cameras that were supposed to be keeping tabs on him were not working. His guards were napping. A man who could potentially bring down governments, royal families, and elites of many stripes is found dead, allegedly of suicide, and the first response from the media is concern this will cause people to circulate conspiracy theories. Never once do they declare that it is their job to get to the truth of the matter, only that they have to help stomp out false narratives. Their job, they proclaim, is to await word from authorities and report what they are told.

I have no desire to try to explain their behavior, only to point out that this is not what news media is supposed to be. Their task—allegedly—is to provide the facts by digging for the facts, not to silence narratives contrary to the official narrative. Just who decides what the official narrative is, anyway? In a healthy society, a little ambiguity and uncertainty is healthy. Only in abusive relationships does someone demand you accept their version of the story without asking questions.

Flash forward to the present. The story is over. Despite the fact that most everyone would like to know more about how Epstein died and about who and what he was involved with, you are likely to hear his name only when a non-employee of the media conglomerates slips "Epstein didn't kill himself" into a live segment.

This is a story people would tune in to watch. The people want the truth about this, this would make the media a ton of money. And if even one mainstream station chose to cover it, every other station and newspaper would be forced to cover it as well.

But nobody is. While the media freely floats conspiracy theories about Vladimir Putin having tapes of prostitutes peeing on Trump, while Tulsi Gabbard is being called a Russian asset without anyone bothering to back it up with evidence, there is a conspiracy of silence surrounding the Jeffrey Epstein story. There is no other option but to call it a conspiracy. How exactly it works or why it exists are not something I can fully explain, nor do I care overmuch to speculate on it. The only thing that concerns me is that the media is acting contrary to their stated and observable interests: to supply truth, generate viewers, and create wealth. It is undeniable that the people want more information and the media is intent on not giving it to them.

Is this the media you are supposed to trust when they tell you there are necessary reasons to send your children off to war? The media you are to trust to tell you that the drugs your kids will be prescribed for the rest of their lives are safe? That the people in charge of our economy are making the best possible decisions for all of us? The media you should trust to ensure your drinking water is safe?

Turn on your television, flip through the channels, and realize that every talking head you come across has made a choice to keep silent about Jeffrey Epstein. Know that all of them are okay with protecting those who have sex with children. Know that whatever banal bullshit they are talking about is more important in their minds than teenage girls being used as sex slaves for the rich and powerful. Understand when they attempt to impart their opinions on current events that they serve the powerful and corrupt, or at least know enough not to speak out against them. For once in your life, get it through your head that the job of understanding the world you live in must be done by you and cannot be left to such people.

You cannot trust those who grow wealthy by keeping silent.

Who grow wealthy by keeping you distracted.

Joy Behar, who insists that she cares about women's issues, and is silent.

Rachel Maddow, who tells you everything is Russia's fault, and is silent.

Sean Hannity, who will warn you about Mexican rapists, and is silent.

Trevor Noah who cracks a joke about the absurdity of anyone who would question the official narrative.

Brian Williams, who tells you how beautiful missiles are, and is silent.

Anderson Cooper, who tells you to trust the system—the same system that allowed Jeffrey Epstein to die in prison—and is silent.

Ellen DeGeneres, who kisses women on TV to prove she's a liberal, and is silent.

Every single person on television who is permitted to address the viewing public is silent.

Ask yourself how they can all stay silent while pedophiles walk free. Not pedophiles merely, but those who turn teenage girls into sex workers. All it would take is for one of them to speak up and demand answers.

And if it all seems quite unbelievable to you, ask yourself why it is you stay silent? Once you realize that you have not spoken up, you will start to understand how such a conspiracy of silence could ever happen, how a society is more concerned with protecting child predators from justice than it is protecting children from the powerful and corrupt. If we can stay silent, if we can stay willfully ignorant or misinformed on this issue, what other lies are we swallowing? What other corruption and abuses of power are we allowing to exist? How many lies and silences are we allowing the media to feed us?

Don't ask how it is possible, simply admit that it is real. Once we as a society have done that, then we can begin to understand how it happened. Then we can begin to bring justice to those who for so long have felt themselves above it. But it will be us, not the people on the television, who will have to break the silence.

When The Media Says ______, They Mean ______.

A lot of people don't follow the news because it's easy to get lost in the details. To make matters worse, those working in the news business tend to develop jargon that is unfamiliar to the rest of us. And of course, there are those in think tanks who like to use particular terms in order to get the desired response from consumers of information. With that thought in mind, I have decided to translate newspeak for the average person in order to help them understand what's going on in the world.

Let's start with a simple phrase you may have been hearing a lot lately: "Blue No Matter Who". To the uninitiated, this might be a little confusing. But if we put it through the translator, we come up with "You're not going to get the candidate you want. We're going to give you a pro-war, pro-corporatist candidate and we want you to be rabidly excited about it." See how that works?

Here's another one: When they say "special analyst for CNN", they mean CIA agent. Same translation applies to special analyst for MSNBC. Got it?

Good, let's try some others. Remember, when they say _____, what they really mean is _____.

Regime ->Any government not doing the bidding of the U.S.

Extreme Left -> New Deal Democrats

Democrat ->Republican

Centrist ->Rightwing

Republican ->Fascist

Journalist ->Propagandist

Traitor ->Journalist

Dead Traitor ->Principled journalist (Arjen Kamphuis, Gary Webb, Daphne Caruana Galizia)

Russian Bot ->Anyone arguing against oligarchy or war

Russian Talking Point ->Peace

Putin Puppet -> Anyone who refuses to be a puppet for the Military Industrial Complex

Hack ->Leak

Bombshell -> A shell without a bomb

Terrorism ->Violence committed by Palestinians

Response ->Violence committed by Israel

Preemptive Response ->Violence with an added adjective

Measured Response ->An Israeli rocket lobbed at a Palestinian kid throwing rocks

Provocation ->Standing too close to an Israeli fence

Proof ->Assertions from anonymous sources within intelligence agencies

Conspiracy Theory ->Logical questions to illogical narratives

Socialist -> Anyone who is inconvenient to the oligarchy

Socialist Dictator ->A leader of a foreign nation who believes the resources of that nation belong to the people rather than transnational corporations

Sanctions ->Siege warfare

Purist ->Anyone opposed to U.S. bombs being dropped on children in other countries or corporations owning our government

Moscow Mitch ->Corporate Mitch

Failed State -> Country we've sanctioned into starvation

Russiagate And The Salem Witch Hunt

(Originally shared on September 4, 2019)

I remember talking to someone at work about a year and a half ago who was sounding me out on politics. I cleared the first hurdle when he asked me if I was a Trump supporter and I said no.

Then he asked me what I thought about the whole Russiagate thing and I was politely dismissive. "There's got to be something to it," was his reply. I knew just what he meant. With all the non-stop talking about it on every media outlet, there had to be some truth to the matter. After all, where there's smoke, there's bound to be fire.

Where there's smoke there's fire is generally a good rule to go by, but for every rule there's the exception. I would clarify by saying where there's smoke, there's fire, except when someone's blowing smoke up your ass. Whether there was any fire (there wasn't), you have got to realize by now that a whole bunch of people have been blowing smoke up the ass of the American public bigtime for the last 2-plus years.

It's hard to imagine how such a nonsensical narrative can spin out of control the way Russiagate has, but the truth is it was never about Russia at all. It was merely a story that happened to serve the interests of several different, extremely powerful, components of our nation. Had it only been of use to one, its impact would have been limited, but it nicely dovetailed so that the Democratic Party, the military industrial complex, the intelligence agencies, and the media all saw ways to advance their agenda. Let me briefly break it down for you:

--The Democratic Party found in Russiagate an excuse for why they lost the election to Donald McDonald.

--The military industrial complex found in it a tool to steer Trump away from his campaign promise to decrease tensions with Russia.

--Intelligence agencies and the deep state found an excuse to do what they've been trying to do for a long time: censor speech on the internet that runs contrary to the official narrative.

--The media found a story that would sell that would involve no actual journalism. For two years all they've had to do is wait to be spoon-fed information by the intelligence agencies and think tanks, spew it back out for their audience, and make wild conjectures about what Putin is up to. No other era of journalism has ever had it so easy, nor made so much money from the wrecking of our nation's democratic institutions.

--Finally, mainstream liberals needed an excuse to stay asleep and continue the pleasant dreams they had been dreaming, nestled in the comfy bed of righteous empire. This was the easiest explanation, requiring no effort, just trust in the institutions to put things right.

Those who reject this explanation see in it a conspiracy theory that would involve too many parts, but in fact the complete opposite is true. I'm not saying these four powerful components of our nation are engaged in an implausible conspiracy theory, I'm saying they're each pitching one, each in order to serve their own interests. Which is not to say that these four different interest groups are not linked in many different ways, just that each has more or less their own reasons for pushing the Russiagate yarn. If they were working closely together to push this story, it might almost have appeared to be coherent.

Take, for example, the Salem Witch Trials. There was one wildly false narrative, around which many different people in the community decided they would buy into in order to serve their own interests. There was no grand conspiracy created by a cabal that determined how everything would play out, there were just a bunch of self-serving parties that recognized an opportunity for personal gain through the advancement of a witch hunt. A depressing but undeniable tendency of human nature. Church leaders sought to squelch dissent, while individual members of the community wished to get rid of people they didn't like. Some people just loved the feeling of power they got from holding listeners spellbound by their stories, while others found ways to curry favor by backing up outrageous claims with even more outrageous claims. There were undoubtedly varying levels of true belief, but that didn't make the assertions any more justifiable.

And then you had a bunch of fearful innocents who trusted those in power more than they should have. But I guess you're not that innocent if you're willing to surrender your personal responsibility as a member of the community to those who wish to rule over you.

I shouldn't have to give you proof that those who burned witches at the stake were wrong in their assertions and their behavior, unless of course you want to argue that witchcraft was actually taking place. I assume we can agree that there were various stupid, selfish, even evil reasons for why such a wild narrative spun so wildly out of control.

I am, however, more than willing to give you evidence of how the Russiagate narrative served the interests of those powerful groups I've mentioned. I've already explained to you what each stood to gain, now let me show you how each got what they wanted.

--The Democrats didn't have to change a God damned thing, or at least they are under the impression they don't. Rather than taking into account the troublesome progressive wing of their party, the one that rejects corporate control and war, they have labeled them useful idiots of Putin every time they say something damaging to corporate Democrats.

--The military industrial complex has managed to get the Trump administration to supply arms to the fascistic government in Ukraine, bomb Russia's ally Syria, roll out yet more crippling sanctions against Russia's ally Venezuela, increase troop presence on Russia's borders, and scrap existing arms deals. They made out really well.

--The deep state and the intelligence agencies have justified telling Facebook and other social media platforms what they will and will not accept. The amount of censorship of the alternative media is profound, and we are yet merely at the starting point. All done in the name of Russiagate.

--Corporate media has had the opportunity to stab at the heart of alternative media, setting themselves up as THE OFFICIAL voice for REAL journalism, even as their reporting reaches all-time lows. Corporate media will never tolerate work done by alternative media, because nobody can be expected to applaud their executioner. The mainstream media knows it is in an existential battle with truths that, once accepted by the average citizen, will destroy them. Russiagate was a godsend and they seized upon the opportunity eagerly.

--Mainstream liberals have been asked to make no sacrifices. They only have to blame Russia, stupid racist Trump supporters, and Susan Sarandon. Their world need not ever change. Democrats, MIC, CIA, and Rachel Maddow will set things to right. Beat Trump in 2020 and it's back to Sunday brunch.

Yeah, it's hard to awaken from a comforting dream, harder still to take responsibility for having participated in such a harmful and untruthful mania. I'm sure it took those living in Salem a long time to come to terms with the damage they'd done. Hell, I'm sure it took generations to work through. But we don't have that option now. We've unleashed more than the killing of a few innocents, we've pushed ourselves further into confrontation with a nuclear-armed nation, a decision that might yet have incalculable costs. Oh, and we've abandoned absolutely every issue that is dear to the Left in order to do it.

"Time to move on", you say. Fair enough, we'll agree to forget the whole burning people at the stake episode. On one condition: Wake the fuck up to the fact that the Democratic Party, the military industrial complex, the intelligence agencies, and the media are not your friends! Then we can move on.

America's Slide Into Infantilism

As children, we have a naïve notion about how when we grow up we will have both the power to change the world and the freedom to do what we please. Then we grow up and we learn about responsibility. At least, most of us learn. It seems that we as a society have been slowly slipping away from the notion of responsibility, at least beyond the paying of bills and showing up to work on time. We still shoulder our individual financial obligations, but beyond personal matters, we have rather fallen away from the whole notion of being grown-ups.

I can't help wondering how other societies see our own, if there are any out there we have not yet infected with the inability to reach a degree of adulthood. For all of recorded history, culture has been maintained and passed down from generation to generation, and in that manner, many cultures have matured into rather sophisticated examples of what civilization can be. Sure, all of them are flawed, just as all human beings are flawed. In many ways, the youthful society that is The United States has set an example of better behavior to those cultures that have been so diligent in clinging to their past. That has always been the beauty of America, but it is also our flaw. And whenever a positive is too much accentuated, the flaw becomes more evident. The more a foundation is built from a flawed concept (as all concepts are), the greater the danger the flaw presents.

America's great flaw and great asset is its youth. It has worked so well as an asset that we have built the entire edifice of our nation upon it. It has worked so well we have led the entire world in unprecedented technological revolutions. We have built something incredibly impressive upon a powerful but untested foundation. And it has for so long stood the test that we have ceased to worry about the imperfection that exists within it (just as imperfection exists within everything).

We have defined ourselves as the new kid on the block, the young rebel. We are the New World, the pioneers that discovered new terrain, at last making humanity a global and interrelated whole. The only problem is, we are no longer young. We are a nation doing a comb-over in order to hide the thinning hair, still trying to fit into the jeans we wore when we were eighteen. We had such a good time in high school and were so popular that we don't want to grow up. But we have to. Our situation has changed. There is no frontier we can send people to when the society we have built becomes intolerable. We can no longer run away, we are now as immobile as Europe has been for quite some time. We have sown our wild oats, it's time to start being responsible.

Unfortunately, we have done just the opposite. So pleased are we with what we once were and so unwilling to face life as it now is, we are regressing. As Gil Scott Heron said nearly forty years ago, "this country wants nostalgia. They want to go back as far as they can - even if it's only as far as last week. Not to face now or tomorrow, but to face backwards." Things have only gotten worse since then. Ironically, our desire to retain our youth and innocence has led to senility.

It isn't just the past that we cling to, any delusional way of seeing life more pleasantly and ourselves more impressively will do. Our movies don't reflect reality anymore, nor does our music reflect our lives (we would have to outdo Sodom and Gomorrah for that to be true). Our news doesn't reflect what is really going on in our nation and the world, and our politicians aren't any better at addressing the issues that most concern us.

And somehow we are all right with that. Because the media and the messengers have done such a good job transforming us into mindless consumers rather than functioning adults. We see the world through the same simplistic perspectives our masters do, a strictly economic one. As teenagers we asked our parents for the keys to the family car without giving any thought about who pays for the upkeep and the insurance and the monthly payments, feeling we have contributed enough by throwing in a few bucks for gas.

Today we feel equally entitled because we pay for it all, but we neglect other costs: how it effects our climate and environment, the military interventions required to ensure cheap and reliable gas, the taxes required to keep the roads in good shape.

Somewhere along the way we stopped growing up and taking on the responsibilities of adulthood, all the while demanding all the privileges. Sports heroes claimed they weren't role models, businessmen denied any responsibilities to the communities in which they worked, and our storytellers abandoned the job of passing on the wisdom of the elders and instead went to work in marketing. We are a country utterly unconnected to the kind of wisdom that requires roots, and we are rapidly headed towards utter infantilization.

It can perhaps best be seen in the political leader of our nation, Donald Trump. It is obvious in his four bankruptcies and just about anything he does that he is utterly unfamiliar with the concept of responsibility. It was no less apparent in the alternative we were given, Hillary Clinton, who never seemed to think herself responsible for anything she had done while in government, from her voting for the Iraq War to her active involvement in the overthrow of Muammar Gaddafi that has left Libya a failed state. Responsibility is for adults, and they are precious few to be found. The cameras of the media do not focus on them because they are not sexy and are no good for selling cars or beer.

We are a nation that never made the step to adulthood and are now rapidly regressing back to the cradle. Our best attempts at politics are no more mature than siblings sitting in the back seat on a long car ride who poke each other and then try to convince their parents it was the other's fault. But there are no parents, and there is no one driving the car except corporations that aren't paying attention to the road but instead are busily digging through the cracks in the seats for whatever loose change might be there.

If we are not already there, we shall soon regress into complete infantilism, capable of nothing more than mindlessly consuming and creating waste. Then there will soon be no adults left who are able or willing to spoon-feed us or change our nappies. Sooner or later, we will have to grow up. Let us hope that occurs before it is too late.

Squirrel

(Originally shared on James Rozoff, Solutionist on May 6, 2018)

I chanced upon our local paper, a USA Today tendril, and was captivated by this headline: The Smell Of Death Still Fills Mosul (Subhead: Bodies of Islamic State terrorists and their victims strewn among the rubble a year after liberation fight). From the article comes this line "Nearly a year after...city liberated from the Islamic State, a putrid odor still fills the air from thousands of corpses left in the rubble." This, more than fifteen years after the United States invaded Iraq under false pretenses. Fifteen years of untold human suffering and catastrophic loss of human life, culture, and history. Being in another country for fifteen years is not war, it is occupation. American children who were then three years of age are now old enough to join in the next major operation that will no doubt occur within the next year or two.

And yet in, all that time, no one has been held accountable for selling a war that has caused so much suffering and had nothing to do with the narrative of Weapons of Mass Destruction that was so arrogantly thrust down our throats by the mainstream media, think tanks, politicians, and intelligence agencies. Nobody who was then in a position of power told the truth, and yet no one in any position of power has been taken from that position. The status quo remains the same. The only difference is that those who lied to us then were promoted while those who told us the truth have been banished from the major arteries of information dissemination. As a result, those who pushed the war have become emboldened by the fact that they suffered no consequences for their criminal behavior. They have been taught the very unfortunate lesson that they can act with impunity, and you can bet it is a lesson that has been learned. Why, even at this moment they are actively en-

Holy shit! I just saw that Russia hacked the DNC emails. WTF? It's true, I just heard it from the Washington Post who quoted anonymous sources within intelligence agencies. I can't believe Russia would-

OMG!!. Russia hacked the Vermont power grid. What the hell is going on?

Okay, never mind about that. Apparently, they didn't—

BUT THEY ARE TRYING TO HACK THE FRENCH ELECTION!!!!!

Okay, I guess the French government said after the election that there was no evidence of Russian interference. Which, I guess if you think about it, means that the U.S. totally influenced the French election by claiming Russia tried to influence the French-

Hold EVERYTHING! This is how insidious the Russian plot to subvert our free and fair election system--which has time after time provided us with the best of all possible candidates--really is. They actually used Pokemon Go to influence voting. Holy shit, there are apparently 13 Facebook trolls saying things about American politics that doesn't jibe with what CNN is telling us, including a picture of a buff Bernie Sanders. RT is allowing people like Chris Hedges and Jesse Ventura to say things and Jimmy Dore and Caitlin Johnstone and Jill Stein and anyone to the left of Hillary are being used as useful idiots by Russia and Russian bots on Twitter are encouraging distrust of our honorable and glorious mainstream media institutions and spreading the absolute falsehood that Uncle Sam loves some of his darker-skinned nephews and nieces less than others and OMG(squared) Russia poisoned a former double agent in Britain and hacked Joy-Ann Reid's blog in order to smear her as a homophobe and...

That's all the time I have for this essay. I'm sorry I went off-topic, but I'm sure you understand my need to do so. Please join me tomorrow as I discuss how the United States armed the very terrorist organizations they told us were existential threats to our very way of life in order to-

Holy Shit! Assad just gassed his own people!!! Change of plans.

Earth-2 News

Picture if you will an alternate Earth, one very much like our own yet with subtle differences. If readers of comic books and pulp sci-fi can do it, it shouldn't be all that hard for you. Imagine a United States much like we know it, only one that was able to transition to the metric system sometime in the late 70s. Maybe that will give you an idea of the fine distinctions we are talking about. Let us play out recent events on their planet in order to imagine our reality, not as it is, but as it might be.

Turn on the television and you will see the same stations, and yet there is something different. You turn to CNN and you gasp to realize you didn't hit them during a commercial break. How often does that happen? You are shocked to find that they are ankles deep in a discussion about climate change, and their guests are neither Hollywood celebrities nor employees of the oil industry. The mere fact they are discussing global warming blows you away, the fact that they are doing so intelligently, listening to expert scientists in the field, leaves you uncomprehending.

You are amazed. You take it all in for a moment, feeling suddenly hopeful about the human race. And then...

You become bored. Oh, it's not your fault, you have been conditioned that way. You have been trained to react emotionally rather than intellectually to important and even not so very important issues. You are trained to direct your anger towards someone and here the discussion is scientific and factual. Worse than that, you are not used to being given information in such dense packets. You keep waiting for a commercial so you can get back to your physiological routine of checking your cell phone or reaching for the remote. You find yourself brought out of your routine and feeling physically uncomfortable.

So you change the channel. Out of habit, out of conditioning. Without any conscious decision-making guiding you, you switch to FOX. Again, you are surprised to find something different than what you expected. You had prepared yourself to feel a sick feeling in your stomach. Indeed, you notice it there now, even though there was nothing to trigger it other than the FOX logo, to which, you realize, you have been conditioned like one of Pavlov's dogs. But you notice there is not the usual attacks coming from the hosts, but instead they are asking their guests to explain themselves more fully. Yes, the host still leans right, but he is respectful and thoughtful. Again, the cognitive dissonance becomes too great and your hand works the remote without the slightest conscious awareness of it doing so.

You are on MSNBC. At least you think it is. But there's something wrong, something very, very wrong. It has been all of twenty seconds now and you haven't heard them say "Russia!" You get the feeling you would get if someone opened their mouth to say something but never did, only stood there with their mouth open, awkwardly. It's like trying to dance to a song in 5/4 rhythm, it just throws you off entirely. But soon they switch to a story you are familiar with, and it gives you something to hold on to. You relax as you see Mark Zuckerberg sitting in front of a congressional committee, and you realize this world isn't so very different from your own.

But it is. You see, when the congressmen ask Mr. Facebook what he is doing to keep fake news off his platform, he does not acquiesce but instead rises to his feet in protest. "It is not my job to limit what my fellow citizens can and cannot read," he says. "God knows I am no authority figure, nor am I aware of any person or entity which should be entrusted with such a great responsibility. You ask me to censor what the average person wishes to share with his friends and family, and I consider that a betrayal of their trust. I have invented, or rather, taken credit for inventing, an incredible tool of communication for the average person, so that they need not rely on media that is concentrated in the hands of a few. I consider my responsibility to my users' freedom greater than any obligation I owe to you."

And thus you spend your morning, flipping out of habit from one channel to another. You quickly notice there is no mention of President Trump because the media on this Earth never made Capitalist Trump into a hero and role model. Indeed, the entire 2016 presidential campaign was covered with a focus on issues rather than ratings.

Yes, Earth-2 is in many ways similar to our own. One important distinction, however, is that the tremendous tools for propaganda are in the hands of those who wish to use them for good rather than evil.

Can you imagine that? Those who now control the propaganda machine can, and they know it is vital for them to silence those voices that would weave a narrative other than the one they have been busy spinning since the dawn of television. The arrival of the internet and social media has given unprecedented opportunity for ordinary citizens to research issues and share information. Because the giant media's role is to support the interests of undemocratic forces (corporations and the Military Industrial Complex), they are doing all they can right now to ensure that they control the narrative. But it is a struggle exactly because the internet provides alternate voices. But if they have their way, dissenting voices will soon be silenced and the powerful opponents of democracy and freedom will sleep more soundly. We must do everything possible to make sure this does not happen.

The Media Is Not Dead, It Is Undead

(Originally published April 2, 2018 on my blog, James Rozoff, Solutionist)

Read the articles in the mainstream papers if you must, but read them carefully. Read them all, but read them not as a letter from a loved one but as information passed on from a stranger whose loyalties and motivations are suspect. Or worse, from someone who has lied to you in the past. Maybe not on unimportant matters but on those issues that matter most.

Read what is written, and ignore the headlines that are thrust at you from every angle. The game they play is to give you so much information you skim along the surface rather than plumb the depths. So when you encounter an argument, engage with it or disregard it. Read carefully, noting as you go how much is mere speculation. Like every other article on Russia and whatever they are being accused of on a particular day, the careful wording is always the same: "insiders (unnamed) say", "suggesting", "probably", "many theories. The most obvious is", "One former senior Foreign Office adviser said:" (another anonymous source from an intelligence agency), etc. It's important that you note this now, because in a month or two this will all be referred to as absolute fact without any additional evidence presented. And it will be strung together with a myriad other articles that do not bear up to a careful read as an indication that so many different assertions cannot all be wrong. In short, assertions soon become incontrovertible fact, and if you dare question what was once an assertion you are labeled a conspiracy theorist, an idiot, and a Russian troll.

For me, each weak argument shouted with great arrogance and confidence and lacking any convincing evidence does not strengthen the overall narrative that is pushed so very hard but does the opposite. I ask myself why serious journalism isn't being done on an issue that is so very important to get right. I wonder why it is that questioning the official narrative is not answered with cogent arguments and undeniable facts but instead with attitude and arrogance. And most of all, I question why each and every article plays upon our lower mental functions rather than our higher ones. If, in fact, Russia poisoned a Russian traitor, is that something that need be responded to immediately? If revenge is a dish best served cold (as some use as a rationalization for why Putin would revenge himself on someone whose relevance has long passed), should we not wait to find the appropriate response to such an action? And more importantly, shouldn't we get the facts right before making an assertion and acting upon it? Is there anything to be lost by getting the story right, and would we not be doing a service to the general public and the notion of an informed citizenry to make sure they are being given the appropriate facts?

What I see is exactly the opposite. We are supposed to unquestioningly accept what anonymous sources from intelligence agencies tell us, and the press passes that off as journalism. It is the job of journalists to question, to be skeptical and to dig for the truth. What I am witnessing bears no resemblance to that. It has all the hallmarks of propaganda. How can you call it anything else? And yet American media smugly point out the flaws of the Russian media as though it were acting out the Biblical parable of the speck and the beam. The difference between Russian media and American media is that Russia shares American media with its citizens in order to show just how absurd it's become. When was the last time American media has done likewise?

I'm going to make a suggestion to you, and you will at first find it ridiculous. Then I will give you my reason for it, and if you find anything ridiculous in it, please share. My suggestion to you is that you watch Russia Today (RT) and listen to Sputnik Radio. I don't suggest that it has no bias, it is just infinitely more intelligent than any other news source you will likely encounter in the United States. Why is that? Because here we have been busy purging our media of anyone who has objected to either war or the propaganda required to make a country go to war. On what television station, newspaper, or radio program can you hear the thoughts of any of the prominent politicians and journalists who opposed either the Iraq War or the justifications used to support it? The list includes Phil Donahue, Chris Hedges, Jesse Ventura, Greg Palast, Pat Buchanan, Dennis Kucinich, Noam Chomsky, and many others. They have been purged from our media in a way that would make Joseph Stalin blush. They were the ones who got the story right, who should have been lauded and promoted. Instead they have been silenced and marginalized. So where does one go to hear from those who have been banished from U.S. media for the crime of being right? RT. Meanwhile, those who got the story absolutely wrong are now pushing the Russian narrative with all the certainty and bullying they once used to push the Iraq War. Does anyone remember how Joe Scarborough was trying to get to the right of Bill O'Reilly on the issue? Does anyone remember the conservative Arianna Huffington's appearances on FOX News? Does anyone care that the same think tank operatives that pushed for the Iraq War are now pushing for unfriendly relations with Russia?

What frightens me the most (besides nuclear war, of course) is that the mainstream media that gets every story wrong is in lockstep with those in the government who wish to silence independent journalists who dare to question the official narrative. The brightest and most questioning minds of the day are being subjected to censorship on many levels, especially if they happen to express an anti-corporate or anti-militarist viewpoint. The media is not simply dead, it is undead, and its only drive is to suck the brains from the skulls of the living. It is an active agent for oppressing the American people and, by extension, the world. A new media must arise that relies on journalists with integrity and a track record of investigation rather than propaganda. Sure, there are a lot of fake stories being pushed out there, but if you allow honest and open debate, the trustworthy will in time make reputations for themselves that will set them apart. But they will never be the big-name multi-million dollar salaried individuals working for mega-corporations we have now. Nobody makes $30,000 a day telling the truth.

The Greater Danger

(Originally posted February 21, 2018 on my blog James Rozoff, Solutionist)

To a surprising degree these days I am amazed by the amount of agreement that exists between intelligent people on the right and those on the left. This leads me to believe there is something very wrong with the center, the mainstream, the official narratives that are only the beliefs of the majority because they are forced down our throats by the major media players.

It's funny how it has taken me over a year to distill my thoughts, observations, and gut feelings into a simple thesis statement, but I notice even the official narrative has never gotten beyond RUSSIA! RUSSIA! RUSSIA! In truth, the mainstream does have a central message it never wavers from, though it does not state it explicitly. It is this: Russia is bad, Russia has harmed us, Russia is our enemy, and we must do something about Russia. Whatever the alleged specifics of the moment, whether it is hacking, colluding, influencing, or whatever, the core message has not changed. Turn on your TV or radio, or read the paper, and that is the message you are meant to receive, no matter the story.

Of course, the media will never explicitly state their central thesis: liars never do. Liars and gaslighters never give you simple and honest answers, they want to keep you in the dark. They want to keep you doubting yourself so that you trust them instead. They want you to hand over to them your personal autonomy so that they can rule you. Oh, you might get a certain illusion of power in the exchange. They will permit you your rage so that you feel like you are accomplishing something, but that rage is only permitted so long as it is directed by them and supports their cause. You will only ever be permitted to punch down, never up at the ones who dictate your reality. Step out of line and you will catch all hell for it. They will demand all the obedience an army drill sergeant does, and you will find it easiest to obey until you no longer realize that that is what you are doing.

It is not your will so much that they shut down as your mind. Once your mind ceases to function logically, critically, and skeptically, your will is easily overcome. Once you react in fear rather than thoughtfully, the natural response is to retreat to safety. As a frightened child retreats to the safety of his parents, so too does the frightened adult retreat to the safety of his government, the flock, whatever source of authority speaks loudly and forcefully and seems to know what's going on and what needs to be done. The mainstream media also fits that bill.

If I make a comparison to Nazi Germany, you will surely object. I merely do so to point out the worst-case scenario for how this sort of manipulation and surrender of rational thinking to fear can occur. I do not say that in this case it will go as far as it did in Nazi Germany, I only say it is going in that direction and no one can really determine how far it will go. But seeing as how we live in an age where weapons are infinitely more powerful than any that existed in World War II, we don't have to go nearly as far in the direction taken by Nazi Germany in order to come up with an unimaginably worse scenario.

I mentioned I finally distilled all my thoughts and observations and fears into a single, declarative statement. It is this: Anyone who ignores the mountains of evidence that our media provides us with willfully deceptive information in order to focus our attention on Russia as an enemy is lacking any sense of proportion.

From there, the rest of the argument springs naturally. But first let me briefly support the central thesis. You can see the evidence elsewhere in my writing. I have constantly pointed out examples of journalism that are not merely incompetent but willfully misleading. I have pointed out the media exhibits a certainty without room for doubt that should never exist in any respectable reporting, a one-sidedness on par with anything Nazi Germany called news. But the primary evidence can be seen simply by turning to your favorite news source. Is it providing you with useful, actionable, accurate and nuanced information? Is it doing a good job discussing and reporting on issues such as global warming and is it giving it the attention it deserves? Did it do a good job reporting on the 2016 Presidential election? Did it do a good job of getting to the truth behind Weapons of Mass Destruction in Iraq or babies being torn from incubators in Kuwait?

If you can honestly answer yes to any of the questions above, then there might be some room to argue against my assertion. Otherwise, you should agree that the primary source of misinformation is our own media and therefore any attempt to place alleged Russian interference (claimed by the very media that is the admitted greater problem) as a primary concern lacks proportionality.

Now back to what can be argued from my central thesis. Anyone who has demonstrated no capacity for proportionality on the Russian interference issue does not deserve our trust. Whether they be willful agents of a skewed perspective or merely mindless bits of driftwood being pulled along in the great flood of the narrative, they clearly lack the capacity for leadership. If we are talking about politicians, they are unworthy of your vote. If they are journalists, they are unworthy of the time you spend reading their reports.

This is not to dismiss the Russian interference story or anyone who believes that such a thing took place. But we need to acknowledge there has been an unprecedented propaganda push that has taken place. It could be argued that a dysfunctional media that sees profit as its only obligation is to blame, but cause is not the immediate concern. That can be sorted out later, the issue we need to address in the moment is that we have a media and political system that must be fixed. Only those in the broken systems, or those who have uncritically accepted their narrative, would say differently.

The Slow Strangling Of Our Consciousness

Asking the experts of today to solve the world's problems is like asking the priests of the volcano god how to end the drought. All they will tell you to do is sacrifice a virgin, it's all they know. Today's experts are little different, there are just more of them. Ask them what their solutions are, and they will tell you to bomb it, privatize it or medicate it.

Everyone in a position of power in a corrupt system is de facto corrupt himself. In bowing to a corrupt authority, they have surrendered their conscience, have proven themselves unable to choose between right and wrong. They cannot save us, they can only hurt us. We must help ourselves, there is no other power we can turn to.

Those in power, whose job it is to inform the public, are more herders of opinion than people interested in expanding our understanding of the circumstances we now face. Their job is to limit the view of those who toil for the present system in the same way horses are blinkered to prevent them being distracted from the task demanded of them.

And in blinkering others, they blinker themselves. Intent on their task, they are so focused on it that they lose sight of their larger obligation to humanity. Not constricted themselves, they yet become even more myopic than those they blinker because, as it is said, none are so blind as those who refuse to see.

An object in motion tends to stay in motion. A rock rolling downhill not only continues to roll downhill, it picks up speed as it does. Media that is more concerned with directing thought than it is opening new paradigms and providing greater context for its viewers will not merely maintain the status quo but will continue to narrow the window through which the world is shown. This has been occurring for decades now, though it has happened just slowly enough that we somehow have not become aware of it. The imperfections of the human mind are many, and the study of how those imperfections can be exploited has been well funded. Kind and decent human beings can be manipulated into supporting the most inhuman of systems if they are led to believe that the "experts" know more than they. Research the Milgram experiments if you have any doubt.

There are two directions thought can travel: outward and inward. We can expand our understanding of the world we live in by permitting ourselves to hold more than one possibility, one paradigm at a time. By not demanding hard and simplistic answers we can drift off into seeing facts and events from multiple perspectives. This requires a degree of faith, a relative absence of fear. In this way we can acquire a more sophisticated and nuanced understanding of the world and our place in it.

But fear is a barrier that bounces such understanding back upon ourselves. The media has erected a curtain of fear that causes us to seek simple answers in order to deal with immediate threats that may or may not be real. The media would have you believe that ISIS, fascists, Russia, Iran, North Korea, and people of the party opposite yours are right outside the door. The crisis is perpetual, though ever-shifting, and in such a situation, you have little recourse but to trust those who have been kind enough to alert you to the threat. They have to run the media this way, it's good for business.

Once your thoughts and perceptions begin to peer inward, once you begin to discard possibilities and instead embrace simplistic solutions, the lens through which you see the world continues to shrink. Like the teeth of a predator, the tools of the media are designed to grab hold of you and constantly direct you towards its awaiting maw. You sit transfixed, staring with fear and incomprehension at the world outside which is actually the world inside the media's constricted narrative.

It is worth reminding yourself that the media is not your friend. What they do they do for money. There are ample examples easily found on the internet where those who are in the know admit as much. The CEO of CBS himself said of Donald Trump's presidential run, "It might not be good for America, but it's damn good for CBS." Are these the sort of people you want guiding you, guiding your nation? Are these the sort of people in whose hands you want to place your emotional and spiritual well-being? The future of the planet?

They do what they do for money. They do what they do for self-enrichment. Oh, I know, the mantra of the day is that the free enterprise system that rewards individual greed ends up being the ultimate delivery system for all that is good for us. It is repeated to us constantly until we accept it uncritically, indeed unthinkingly. And who is it delivering that message to us night and day? The media, which is a conglomeration of corporations that not only seek profit for themselves but seek a cultural milieu that justifies such profiteering for themselves and their sponsors.

The result is ultra hi-def television that nonetheless offers us only black and white broadcasting, the contrast level turned so high that there is little to no gray area. The definition our televisions are capable of is nothing short of miraculous, and yet so little detail is ever provided. Instead, instances of violence are looped continuously and the narrative that accompanies the video must play to the beat.

In short, the media is a Frankenstein monster created by powerful corporate interests and faithfully obedient to the Military Industrial Complex. It is the more direct weapon of those same corporate interests. It has a job, and it is not to inform you. It has a mission statement, and it is not the search for truth. It has an obligation to someone, and it is not the viewer. Unless you truly believe you live in a free society, you must know this is true.

You do know it is true. On some level you are unable to accept the lie. In your calmer moments, those moments where the media is not busily herding ideas that have strayed too far from the official narrative the way a sheepdog herds the flock, you have admitted as much. But then the powers that be find some new unsavory business to attend to and the media is put into motion once again in order to justify some great evil, such as destroying the environment or bombing nations that have done nothing to us. Then the fear sets in and you cling to the narrative the media spins the way Harlow's lab monkeys clung to their cloth mothers.

It's time to step away from the artificial zone of comfort the media has constructed for us. Not only is it a trap, but it is one that crushes us once we are inside it.

It will seem like madness at first, because you have been conditioned your whole life to think within the box. Those paths to death and destruction are the only ones we've been shown, and you've been corrected every time you've strayed too far from them.

But one only has to look honestly at the ever-shrinking mindset that the authorities present to realize it offers no hope to humanity. It offers death, fear, and environmental destruction. Their hope for the future is a technology bereft of all morality or humanity, Their hope is that perhaps we can export a few fortunate ones to some new planet to begin again this dysfunctional system. Hope for tomorrow is just another product or viewpoint they're trying to sell, not a guiding principle.

We're on our own. Humanity must evolve or perish. The system that exists today, the one all the authorities and institutions promote in order to advance themselves, is a death cult hell-bent on wasting Earth's precious resources to make weapons in order to blow up more of Earth's precious resources. Where are the voices in government, in business, or the media that decry the insanity? They are not merely silent, they are loudly crying for more.

A Deconstruction Of The Phrase "Russia Attempts To Hack Our Democracy"

I read this phrase recently—probably for the thousandth time—but the sheer idiocy of it finally struck home. The phrase is this: "Russian attempts to hack our democracy." It has been bothering me for a while now, but sometimes it takes a while for inanity to cross the Rubicon. Roll it upon your tongue for a moment: "Russia attempts to hack our democracy". Taste it if you can, see if you can find any depth or substance in this cotton candy assertion. To anyone with a sophisticated palate, the unusual pairings are rather jarring.

Let's break it down, if we are capable of such an effort. Like a McDonald's cheeseburger, it can appear quite acceptable to one who doesn't much think about what one is consuming. But let us be connoisseurs of message for a moment, let us think about what it is we are digesting. Let us study the relatively simple phrase in its component parts, explore what the symbols mean to us.

Russian. The word is replete with associations. It has always been synonymous with the Soviet Union in the minds of anyone older than thirty and younger than a hundred and ten. The U.S. had always been the home team and the U.S.S.R. was (for anyone outside New York) the Yankees. They were the Ivan Drago to our beloved Rocky. They are the destroyers of freedom. They are, pure and simple, THE ENEMY! They are and always will be Mordor, the evil empire, the land to the east that is by its very existence a threat to all free peoples. One wonders why God or Tolkien saw fit to create such an abomination. We would all be better off if cartographers simply omitted it from any future maps.

"Russian hack". What does this mean? Is hack the right word? Did Russia use sophisticated computer technology to change voting? Was it more damaging than the purging of African Americans from the electoral process through voter ID laws or sub-par equipment and limited access in lower-class neighborhoods? If it was not, why is the media ignoring such issues in favor of Russian hacking? Don't they want what's best for us?

Is it more relevant to our lives as Americans than the billions of dollars poured into our elections from special interest groups that determine the policies that their bought candidates do not write but rather copy into law? Is it more relevant to our elections than the fact that every single major political aspirant must genuflect before AIPAC, Israel's lobbying group?

What do they mean by hacking? What does the word "hack" mean? What exactly does Russia stand accused of? For God's sake, how can we prevent it from happening again if we don't know what "it" is? I guess the lesson is that our secret intelligence agencies will take care of it and that we only need trust them. But it makes me wonder: how can we trust them to take care of the problem when they weren't able to prevent it in the first place? It makes me wonder why they even bothered to bring it up at all if they are giving us no actionable information. "The Russians hacked our election. We want you to know that, we want you to know we are on it, and that what is most important is that you trust us unaccountable agents of security agencies." Doesn't spy stuff go on all the time without the need to reveal such shenanigans to the public? Why then did they feel the need to share this one?

It's frustrating to place all the responsibility in the hands of the intelligence agencies. As a United States citizen I want to do something to help secure our democracy, something more than wearing a pussy hat and Russia-bating (sic) in groups that appear larger on

CNN than they do in person. I feel like someone trying to fight terrorism with plastic sheeting and duct tape. It doesn't make sense to me.

If we have a problem with our elections being hackable, shouldn't we be taking concrete actions to ensure that it is more difficult for it to happen next election? Why in God's name aren't our elected officials scrambling to pass laws that require paper ballots that are hand-counted rather than using hackable computers? Questioning Trump's involvement can wait until we've taken control of our systems back from the Russians. Why are we doing nothing? Don't we care?

If our elections are hackable, shouldn't we have been concerned about this before now? If Russia was able to hack our elections, might not other powerful agents do the same? Perhaps even one or two of our intelligence agencies might think it a good idea to do such a thing. If they did, who would alert the media to the hacking? If, say, the CIA decided to hack our elections, would anybody know? If right now the media is doing no actual journalism on the validity of Russian hacking claims other than passing along information from intelligence agencies, how could we ever expect our media to ferret out the information if such an action took place? If our elections were to be hacked by intelligence agencies or other nefarious domestic groups, wouldn't we want Russia to release the facts to us?

Which once again makes me return to asking what is meant by hacking. Does it mean releasing accurate and truthful information gathered through unsecured e-mail servers? Does it mean revealing inconvenient truths about what is really going on in our country, the way Radio Free Europe once provided a counter narrative to the citizens of the Soviet Bloc?

I worry about the very vagueness of the expression "Russian Attempts To Hack Our Democracy". It is a statement written with an unsharpened pencil and it is hard to read. And vagueness is the tool used by those who would like to get you to believe in something without explicitly saying anything. It is the way Iago talked to Othello about Desdemona, feigning concern for a friend while sowing unfounded suspicions designed to destroy him.

But perhaps it is the use of the word "democracy" that confounds most of all. The word just seems to have an air of purity to it, doesn't it? Democracy is one of those core values, a sacrosanct institution whose virtue needs protecting from debauched men looking to stain its innocence. Accusing someone of hacking democracy contains within it associations of raping a virgin. Our minds rebel at the very thought of it, and our reason goes out the window. We become brutes willing to do anything to protect our women folk. Democracy is an archetypal principle at once vague and yet all-encompassing. It embodies all that is good, and it is enshrined within our most holy of temples. To imagine a foreign power penetrating so deeply into our holiest of holies demands that we defend it at all costs or lose our very identity as a people.

If only we had such an institution. Democracy—at least that which we now call democracy—is not a vestal virgin but a seasoned prostitute. Russia has no need to hack, spy, or subvert. The U.S. government is quite simply up for sale to the highest bidder, and she has no biases whether she sleeps with a local or a foreigner. It is all about the money.

And as far as hookers go, the U.S. government is not especially high priced. Russia has enough money to buy a few well-positioned congresspersons should it so desire. Granted Saudi Arabia is a wealthy John, but it has the U.S. doing things that would make most harlots blush. After all, a prostitute only sells what is hers to give, while a politician makes his money giving away that which does not belong to him. Even children are not safe from such business deals.

Israel too has been frequenting the Capital Hill whorehouse for decades, tossing bills on the pillow for the permission to have its way with Palestinians of all ages. United Arab Emirates plopped down $14.2 million in 2013 and apparently liked the treatment it received, namely a $2 billion weapons sale. And for a mere $2.5 million they got former Attorney General John Ashcroft to work for them, though whether he will be required to wear high heels and garter is not exactly clear.

According to a New York Times investigation (Foreign Government Contributions to Nine Think Tanks, September 7, 2014), "Foreign governments and state-controlled or state-financed entities have paid tens of millions of dollars to dozens of American think tanks in recent years." According to the Times, the highly prominent and influential Atlantic Council received between 5 and 20 percent of its funding from foreign governments. Oil rich nations like United Arab Emirates and Qatar make up 12% of the funding of the

Brookings Institution, which brags that it "has been at the forefront of public policy for more than a century." Dozens of nations from every continent have made it on the list of those contributing to U.S. think tanks which influence U.S. foreign policy, although oddly enough Israel did not make it on the list

Why then would Russia risk war with the most powerful military in the world when it could simply buy what they wanted like everyone else? Why get the John after you to break your legs when for a modest fee you could have your kinkiest fantasies satisfied? Why "hack" when one could "contribute"? Doesn't that sound so much better?

This was my quick dissection of the message. Notice that I make no mention of the messengers. That is a subject I've mentioned in other posts, notably in the essay following this one.

Syria, Russia, And What I Can Say With Certainty (Part 3)

(Originally published April 15, 2017 on my blog James Rozoff, Solutionist)

It came without warning like a force of nature, a tsunami crashing upon the land, sweeping all other concerns away. It was like a sudden lightning storm in the dark of night, making clear what was previously obscure. Yet there was a sense of coordination to it, perhaps more like a blitzkrieg than thunderstorm. One moment everything was in the shadows, the next everything so clear, so fully certain.

And fear. Although we were oh so very certain of so much, fear was nevertheless part of the equation. We were simultaneously absolutely certain of many facts while possessing a gaping hole in our knowledge where our worst fears could reside.

I refer to the revelation of Russian hacking, where in no time at all the story became the story of stories, driving everything else from our consciousness. The media only broke from the story to report on Syria, which only further highlighted the insidious nature of the Russians.

The source of all this certainty and fear, at least initially, was unnamed. Sometimes this source was an unnamed intelligence insider, sometimes the source was an anonymous senior congressional staffer. Here is an example (from January 5, 2017) of the typical news article headline reporting on Russian hacking (NBC News In this case):

<u>U.S. Has ID'd Russians Who Gave Hacked Emails to WikiLeaks</u>

The source was listed in the title as "U.S." The article itself contains many different esteemed sources without ever giving a name or face to any of them. Instead, sources are referred to in this manner: ". A senior U.S. intelligence official with direct knowledge," "The U.S. has also identified," "The source," "said the official," "The staffer," "**The U.S.** has also identified Russian actors who turned over stolen Democratic material to WikiLeaks, **the source** told NBC News," "The official," "Two top intelligence officials with direct knowledge," et cetera, ad nauseam.

This is not journalism, this is not even reporting. This is simply putting into print press releases sent from government agencies. Yet they somehow needed three reporters' names on the byline. What exactly did each of them do?

As far as I'm aware, not a single news agency did any actual investigation into the matter. They simply reported what was told to them by government officials, reported the narrative and in the process swallowed it whole. In the weeks and months that have now followed, never once did I witness in any mainstream American news outlet any sort of critical questioning of the official narrative. It was simply accepted as fact.

Never in the history of germs, conspiracy theories, or cute puppy videos have I ever seen anything spread so quickly, and so authoritatively.

Well, that's not quite true. I have seen this sort of behavior on the part of the media before, many times in fact, though the previous practice has obviously made for perfection. It was the very likeness of those other examples that made me question the Russian hacking story, even more than the story's inherent flaws.

I have seen it played out before, in the build-up to wars. I have seen it played out when we wished to demonize a country or a government. I have seen it every time our government is about to do something very bad and knows it needs to invent justifications for why they are doing it.

Usually such media blitzes are accompanied by first-hand accounts of babies being killed. Usually words like "genocide" or "WMD" are used to pepper arguments that are strong on emotion and weak on facts and logic. But as such typical propaganda tools didn't seem to apply, we relied on unflattering pictures of Vladimir Putin to become a focus for our rage. His very Russianness was enough for us old enough to remember Rocky IV or Rambo III (you remember, when Rambo went to help the heroic "freedom fighters" in Afghanistan, those same types who later killed little girls for trying to go to school, who blew up statues of the Buddha and harbored the likes of Osama Bin Laden. Those freedom fighters are still alive and well today, fighting our enemies in Syria as they once did in Afghanistan).

It turns out it's not the strength of the argument that counts but the conviction in the voice of those who deliver it and the frequency of times it is delivered. Cults indoctrinate members by surrounding them with people repeating the same message while cutting recruits off from those who might tell them something different. The Russian Hacking story is a similar case where the story was everywhere at all times while any voices to the contrary were made to seem like Russian propagandists or ignorant, racist Trump supporters.

I suppose that's why the story caught hold in the more liberal sections of the population, among those who despised Donald Trump and could not fathom how Hillary could be likewise despised by anyone with morals and a brain. Surely Russian hacking is the only possible explanation.

Besides, what if it is true? What if the Russians did hack our election and managed to get their chosen candidate elected? If this is the case, then surely all of the fear is warranted. Isn't it only common sense that the media spend so much time getting to the truth on an issue of such importance?

Perhaps, but that is not what the media is doing. It is not attempting to unearth facts and string them logically into different possible narratives. The media is merely repeating what certain government agencies are leaking to them. Many, often the ostensibly most "progressive", are amplifying it. Funny, but I can no longer recall what Rachel Maddow used to talk about before the Russian hacking story came along.

In short, the only thing the media has done was to foster panic and hatred. It has used the Russian hacking story as a focus for all the hatred Hillary voters are feeling while ignoring all the horrible things Trump is doing. The Democrats have now become the party of war and imperialism and they just don't seem to see anything wrong with that.

Thank God for the deep state. They are the heroes in this narrative. The cry is that something must be done and the only people who can possibly get us out of the crisis we're in are those anonymous, unaccountable government agents who want what is best for us. We must surrender thoughts of being in charge of our own government in moments like these. We must relinquish control to the experts who have selflessly prepared their whole lives for a situation like this. Once the crisis has passed, they will gladly cede the power they have temporarily taken on as a burden. The only thing you need concern yourself with now is maintaining a proper amount of fear and helplessness.

That is the argument being given by the deep state. Not only does the media not question it, it wholeheartedly endorses it. I have a different take. I believe there is never a good time to panic, and there is never a good time to refrain from critical thinking. One needs to keep one's head, especially in a crisis. When a group foregoes reason and abandons themselves to the herd mentality, that is when things go horribly wrong. That is when people stampede each other in an attempt to escape a burning building. It is when economies collapse because of runs on the market. It is the start of wars.

Human beings should never forsake their higher faculties in troubling times, nor should the media ask them to. While we're at it, there is never a good time for the media to abandon their central tenets, their standard operating procedures and their principles. Which brings me to the point of this post.

In the first two parts of this three-part blog, I laid out what I was not sure of, whether Russia hacked or Syria gassed. Now it is time for me to speak of what I know with certainty. When the government has an agenda to push—a goal it is intent on achieving—it is then that the illusion of an independent media dissolves. When called upon, the media abandons its alleged commitment to objective journalism in favor of channeling the official line. Of that there can be no doubt. Never have I seen it work otherwise. It seems to be a universal law that power wins out over principle.

NPR, The New York Times, CNN, etc., they all capitulated to the official story that had at its source anonymous officials from private and unaccountable government agencies. They did not do what news organizations are supposed to do, which is dig for the truth and corroborate testimony.

There is not a single reason for the failure of the U.S. media, nor a heavy-handed power that is easy to point to. Don Henley made it all too clear in his song Dirty Laundry just how vapid TV news was in 1982 and it has rapidly gone downhill since then. Where once news sources made some pretense of putting truth over profit, now, just as in every other field, profit is the only justification for anything. It would be foolish to believe that the same media that obsesses about Caitlyn Jenner can switch gears when an important story arises. Talking heads are cheaper than hiring a staff of investigative journalists, and a whole lot less troublesome.

There are few independent media outlets anymore, institutions that aren't funded directly or indirectly by powerful interests. There are some real investigative journalists still out there but they have been pushed to the edges. Now those edges are being labeled "fake news" by those who wouldn't know news if it bit them. Journalists who practice the long-established craft are either forced to beg for contributions like Greg Palast, or have gone to work for RT like Chris Hedges. Do your country a favor and throw a few bucks in the tin cup of one of the last of the old-time journalists. Donate.

Journalism is dead. What they now call news is whatever they feel will draw and keep the interest of viewers for their advertisers. Investigation is expensive, while talking heads from the pentagon are willing to come in and recite the official position for free. War is profitable, not only for the weapons manufacturers but for ratings as well.

I can't tell you if Russia was in any way involved in the hacking of the 2016 presidential election, nor can I tell you if President Assad used Sarin gas on his own people. The information is not available to me. The mainstream media has no interest in delivering the information citizens require to make the best decisions for ourselves and our country. Of that I am quite certain.

Truth Matters, Your Simplistic Beliefs Do Not

We are in a post-truth world. It is not because the world has gotten so complex, it is not because modernity makes truth subjective, nor is it due to social media. It is because truth is no longer a priority for us. We've become so used to accepting lies that we no longer have the capacity for discerning what is real and what is fake, what has merit and what is without substance.

We live in a world where spin is in the very air we breathe. We are bombarded by advertising nearly every waking moment, and advertisement has no interest in giving an honest or balanced perspective. Though I am probably wrong, I can't help thinking television has more ads than content, each ad pushing an agenda, an agenda which is not the pursuit of truth. And the programming itself must not in any way countermand the essential ideas the ads are pushing or else the advertisers will withhold their business.

Turn off the television. You will still be surrounded by the distortions of those trying to affect the way you perceive the world. Use your cell phone to Google something and you will be subject to advertisement, though most times you won't recognize it as such. While you may be annoyed by the delays caused by ads on YouTube, you likely won't even notice them when on Facebook.

Take a drive and try to unwind. The radio is there to sell you something, and it's not appealing to your desire for truth and reason. Turn the radio off, and you still won't be able to avoid the billboards, even though you may not be consciously aware of them. You think you're not affected but they wouldn't spend billions of dollars for access to your mind if they weren't confident of achieving the intended result. While not interested in truth, they are very alert and in tune when it comes to return on investment.

Lies, spin, and distraction are the building blocks of our culture. Money and power warp truth the same way time and space are bent by gravity.

Facts are no longer pieces we assemble in order to build a better picture of the truth but instead are stones that we can load into our slingshot and fling at others. The idea of a greater, knowable and understandable truth has become a foreign concept to us. Our political discussions are no longer between two sides earnestly attempting to get to the truth but cheap theatrics or gladiatorial combat.

Why? Is it because we are the first generations to come to grips with the cold hard truth that reality is unknowable? Have all previous attempts to understand the world we live in been vain attempts by more naïve and less worldly societies than our own? I guess the answer would be yes for those who don't wish to do the hard work of winnowing their way closer to truth and a firmer grasp on our world. It is the easy answer, the kind that helps us avoid making difficult choices and being in control of our lives. It's much easier to accept what is given to us by the propaganda machine and the politicians bought by moneyed interests that don't have your best interests at heart.

Do we search for truth when it comes to politics nowadays or do we look to be persuaded by those who are telling us what we want to hear? Because what we want to hear is not the truth but the lies. Republicans just want to hear about the lies of the Democrats, and the Democrats just want to hear about the lies of the Republicans. And if you're like me, you see the lies of both. But nobody seems to see the truth when it is spoken. Nobody's interested in it. Who could stand the idea that no matter what side you're on you still need input from the other side? That you still need to balance your point of view with one different from your own? Simplicity. That's what we want, and the best way to achieve that is to allow some authority to tell us what to think.

You see, if you start listening—and not only listening but really looking for the truth in what the other side has to say—then you have to start living in a more complex world. Because while we can reach more closely toward truth than we are now doing, we never actually arrive at it. Truth is something bigger than can ever be stuffed inside our tiny little skulls. To seek truth is to have to admit we don't know everything, and that sometimes we have to add a third option between the true and the false, a holding stage where we keep ideas until we have further evidence. We would need to accept ambiguity, and in accepting ambiguity, we would need to accept intellectual humility.

Fundamentalism is a much easier way of seeing the world. Choose a simplistic idea and have your every observation be colored by it. Facts then no longer sting when you are hit by them. You simply choose the ones you wish and dismiss as lies those that cause discomfort.

That is the point we are now at. One side is incapable of listening to the other side because if they do they might be inconvenienced. They might be taken out of their comfort zone, forced to confront unpleasant and complex ideas to which there are no easy answers.

We've been doing it for a while now. Once you start down that path, and once you start veering from the truth in favor of ideology, you get further and further from the truth. And the further you deviate from the truth, the more you depend on your simplistic ideology to keep you feeling secure. It's a vicious cycle that never ends well. It's the same sort of magical thinking that a drug addict uses. Slowly they cut ties with those who tell them they are living in denial. They seek the company of other drug addicts, who won't tell them their behavior is destructive. They build around them a protective bubble for safety.

But such protection is illusory and temporary. Without a widespread foundation, a tower will surely fall. Similarly, belief systems established on a single viewpoint will also come crashing to the ground. Trying to base your understanding of life on one point of view is like trying to sit on a one-legged stool. You need balance, you need perspective. You need to weigh one point of view with another.

Our fundamentalism, the kind preached by those in places of power today, is capitalism and an actual religious belief that the "magic of the free market" will provide all of humanity's needs. This fundamentalism requires us to disregard all the other foundations upon which societies have been built throughout history. Responsibility to others, civic duty, religious principles, they are either dismissed altogether, given mere lip service, or else twisted into some freakish semblance of their true shape in order to have them fit into the dominant, simplistic paradigm.

On some level we see through the lies we are told. We yet retain some memories of and appreciation for the morals and viewpoints we once held, that have been held by any healthy society on the ascent. On some level we know we are living a lie. But that which we sense is in conflict with that which we are told, and the messaging of the media is so pervasive it tends to silence our inner voice. The silencing of our inner voice leads to irrationality, denial, anger, avoidance.

It is time to abandon the simplistic ideologies that lead us further and further from reality. It is time to tear through the curtain that we have placed over the window so we don't have to face the truth. It may be unpleasant but it is the only way that will lead us from the dungeon of delusion in which we've been living. One way or another the truth will eventually come crashing through our cocoon of fantasy we've been spinning, it is best we make the choice to emerge from it on our own. Only in that way can we achieve the metamorphosis necessary to rise and meet our future.

Which Side Are You On, David's or Digital Capitalist Goliath's?

(Originally shared on September 4, 2021 on Medium)

What the digital revolution did was enable everyone to be an artist, a journalist, pundit, writer, shaper of opinions, with a potential to grow a substantial audience without the need for corporate backing or approval. What it simultaneously did was give corporations an opportunity to spy on us and consolidate power in new ways and on unprecedented levels. It was only a matter of time before the two opposites collided. In truth, the former was only ever permitted in order that people would not focus on the latter. It really was remarkable to connect with independent musicians and contribute to their ability to make music. It was inspiring to see independent authors gain huge readerships (and royalties) without the need for a publishing company telling them what kind of product they needed to create. It was revelatory to see independent journalists show just how completely out of touch corporate politicians and corporate media really were.

We should have known this would never be allowed to continue. It should have been obvious that ordinary people were taking not only profits from corporations but also bypassing the narrative they need to control things. Corporations don't operate on the principle of fairness or philanthropy. Taking money from their shareholders and shaping a world where corporations don't control not only the means of production but the very way people see and interact with the outside world is not an idea corporations are going to be okay with. It was just a matter of time before they would strike back.

Like I said, we should have known. And on some level, most of us did know. It's just that we were being flooded by so much free content and so much potential to reach out and interact freely with others. It was hard not to indulge ourselves, hard not to dive in to all that freedom and exploration and community-building that was busting out all over the world. The internet was such a wonderful creation, and it is only natural that we took advantage of all that it provided.

That's the way the capitalistic system works. They lure you in with free quality product and then once they have you hooked they change the terms. It doesn't matter if we're talking about a drug dealer or the History Channel, they start out by acting like they're your friend and then they end up offering you nothing but Pawn Stars and Ancient Aliens.

Corporate mega-players like Google, Facebook, Twitter, and others, could never have continued to provide you with freedom and a level playing field forever. It would have meant signing their own death warrant. The system they are part of, the system they serve and that serves them in return, could never exist in a free and open environment.

We were sold a David and Goliath story, one where independent artists and voices were given the opportunity to take on the big guys in a fair fight and let the audience decide who they wanted to listen to or watch or read. We were told how we could build up a group of followers on social media we could sell our ideas and our work to and we could build communities that would change the future.

That was the promise. Never, never ever, even if they pinky swear, believe the promises of a corporation or a corporate system. They're the same people who sold you cigarettes and white bread and wars and many things we're not allowed to talk about now without the fear of censorship by algorithms or banishment.

Censorship. It's a word we were frightened to death of a decade ago. Sure, we permitted government agencies to spy on us after 9/11, so we couldn't plot in secret to do things the government might disapprove of, but we could still speak freely in the open any ideas that precluded violence. But spying alone proved insufficient. People talking openly about ideas outside the corporate narrative was poking too many holes in that narrative. So all that freedom and opportunity we were given by the grace of corporate entities was destined to be taken away by those very same entities.

We should have known we weren't simply being given a gift. We should have known like the Trojans should have known when the Achaeans wheeled up a giant horse for them to take into their city that our enemies hadn't suddenly become our friends. But I guess vanity and the sacrifice of eternal vigilance and the beauty of the gift all played their part.

The battle is on. I know what side you were on twenty years ago when corporations were saying we were headed towards a revolutionary new way of doing things. I know you were looking forward to a world where everything was not top down and the little guy could succeed by saying things that resonated with others and by providing product that others wanted to pay for.

But what side are you on now? Are you still with the average Joe, the independent voice and artist, or are you on the side of the corporations looking to silence the voices of the little people who grew too bold?

Don't fold on me now. Don't abandon the ideal of a future where the average person can take on the big corporations and the world can be shaped by ideas rather than money and power. They're going to come up with all kinds of reasons why you need to do so. They are going to make you afraid in any way possible in order to manipulate you and make you go along with what you would never do otherwise, and what you never would have imagined going along with twenty years ago. Don't do it.

The battle is upon us. Which side are you on?

The Media And Elections

(Originally shared on April 13, 2016 in my blog James Rozoff, Solutionist.)

Remember that no matter how much you may dislike a given candidate, the real enemy is the media. The media is the god to whom all bad candidates pledge obedience. As much as candidates try to play the media, in the end it is always the media that plays them.

I even feel sorry for Donald. Seriously. Watching Chris Matthews goad Trump into making an inane comment (as if he needed encouragement) was hard to watch. Donald, even Donald, was trying to avoid a nonsensical question, but eventually Matthews wore him down and got the sound bite he wanted.

Hillary too. I'm not talking about conservative talk show radio, which does an unspeakable butcher job on her while not dealing with the relevant issues that they could actually pin her to the wall on. I'm talking about the mainstream media. No matter how Hillary tries to portray herself, the media always paints her unsympathetically.

Of course, while I feel sorry that they are both victims of the media, they are both also guilty of playing the game. Instead of trying to put forward an appearance that the media will accept, she should worry more about being herself than projecting the right image. And Donald Trump has been playing a game this whole time, knowing how base and immoral the media is that they will lap it up like the sick puppies they are. He had to have known, or should have known, that eventually the media would turn on their favorite circus monkey once the routine got old. Live by the media, die by the media.

Perhaps with this current presidential campaign, though, the populace is finally starting to get it. Perhaps they see that the problem is not so much the candidates but what the candidates have to do to get the attention of the media. I truly believe that the citizens, both liberal and conservative, have finally realized the most corrupting influence on politics today: a media that prefers sound bites to substance so that they have more time for commercials. News organizations that feel no moral obligation to actually report the truth but to bring in more viewers by titillating their audience. Perhaps with the advent of the internet, we are so flooded with click-bait that we now feel we have to sort through all the nonsense in order to find what is meaningful to our lives.

It is the media that has made the election cycle the cesspool it has become. If the media were doing their job, they would winnow out the wheat from the chaff rather than throwing it all on the fire in order to create spectacle. The media is interested in one thing, and that is money. To that end they reduce the amount of reporters they have to pay, avoid controversial issues that they would have to commit to, and accept news uncritically from whatever source is willing to give it cheaply, no matter how untrustworthy they may be. Thus the government, corporations, any powerful figures—the exact people journalism is supposed to protect us from—are able to use the media as its mouthpiece.

Conservatives have learned how untrustworthy the mainstream media is, though they seem less aware that they face the same issue with conservative media. And I really do believe a new generation, one which is perhaps a little more media savvy, realizes the media is nothing more than a device for promoting mindsets the powerful interests want us to embrace. Perhaps it is a little more difficult for us who are older, because we remember media that was able to give us, if not truth, then at least scraps of honesty and bits of enriching programming. But we too are getting to the end of our rope.

It's not over yet. The media doesn't realize how far from reality or the needs of the people it has gone. In the next few months you will see all the skill of the corrupt media on display as it spins out its poisonous web of useless and misleading information.

It will present for you a final freakshow that will leave Jerry Springer and Marilyn Manson envious.

But it's breaking down. No structure built on such shoddy foundations that seeks to reach so high can last for long. True, the damage it will cause as it crashes will be severe, but we'll all be better off once it has fallen.

Beating The Big Boss

I can't help getting the feeling we're playing a video game, and we've worked our way up to the big boss in the last battle. Our thumbs are worn out from pressing the X button a million times and the boss is throwing everything it can at us. Then, all of a sudden, it starts going through all these weird motions like it's going to throw a giant attack at us that will destroy everyone and mean game over. But really it's just going through its death throes and is unraveling right in front of our eyes.

The big boss in this instance is the media, which has spent the last couple of years throwing everything it could at you in an attempt to overwhelm you. But the attack seems to be working less, even as its intensity increases. You can sense it in the eyes of the newscasters (spellcasters) who seize up when they are presented with someone who says they don't believe the official narrative. The look in their eyes is like that of a robot which is confronted with a situation for which it has not been programmed.

All of us, really, are no different. Which is why it is understandable that we feel frightened. Because unlike a video game, things don't end when you beat it but you then have to move on to the real task of replacing the system you have worked so hard to destroy. Once you beat the fake game you have to deal with real life, and most of us would rather not get to the ultimate foe and so have to get off of our couches.

I am terrified of what may come once the established paradigm is overthrown, because as bad as it is, it has provided a degree of security and comfort. Granted, it is the kind of comfort one feels in a luxury vehicle that is speeding towards a cliff, but the human mind is reluctant to surrender that sort of comfort, reluctant to build something new when what we had was so good, at least to those in the driver's seat.

The truth is, we don't know what will come next. We only know that what presently exists is racing us toward extinction. We can choose the comfort of the known, which is an immature way of reacting to the world, or we can choose to leap from our place of safety with a hope that we will be able to respond in a way we never have before. Like a baby bird leaving the nest. Because we must. Because life does not wait until we are ready. Because perhaps we will never decide we are ready on our own. Because that is the way of all living things, to reach outward and go forward. If they are to survive. And I want to survive. Not just for another moment, not just so I can live out my life with a comfy couch and a TV and a video game console to play my pretend life. I want to survive in a much more meaningful way. I want to have children who will outlive me, want them to have children, and so on into an unknown and unknowable future.

Plus, I just really, really want to beat the big boss.

Conclusion

All my life, I've felt myself to be an outsider to the culture that was being fashioned for us by the media. I was born in 1966 to parents who were born in 1923 and who were a generation older than the parents of most of my friends. They were not "hip," had not been raised in a post-scarcity world, nor did they have a TV in their home for the first thirty years of their lives. My parents were "out of touch" children of the Great Depression who never really adjusted to the values being promoted by advertisers in the media.

My siblings—older than me by a decade—were highly influenced by the counter-culture, which rejected the materialism and the commercialism that flowed from the media. From my earliest memories, my ears were filled with music that never got played on the radio, my eyes had access to images and words not seen in the establishment press.

As a result of these influences, I rejected most of the television programming and the pop sensibilities that were fed to my generation as I was growing up. In most every way, I saw the mainstream media as an enemy that used pop culture to drown out far more meaningful and beautiful art, music, and literature.

And yet, the media got its hooks in me. At some point in my life, I discovered not only that I wanted a pair of Nike shoes but that some part of my psyche desperately needed them. I pestered my parents until they bought me a pair, and when I walked into school the next day, I felt finally as if I belonged. That I was worthy. That I was somebody. Because of a pair of shoes.

It seemed that all the fearless individualism I felt in my youth had withered as I reached puberty and the process of making myself desirable to the opposite sex began. The process of separating myself from my parents and becoming a man made me search for values separate from theirs. I felt the need to see how I could stack up against the norms society had set. I needed to prove, as I once had in baseball and football, that I could compete against my peers.

What I did not seem to notice or care about at that time was that much of the game I was playing had been written by advertisers and marketers. Not only did I have to compete in terms of strength, ability, intelligence, and personality, I had to at least in some degree fit the mold the media had constructed for us. It wasn't enough to be a decent person or a clever conversationalist, one had to know the cultural touchstones of a commercial culture based in consumerism and banality.

So I needed Nikes. Perhaps my contemporaries would have accepted me without them, but I wouldn't have felt as though I belonged otherwise. I learned to buy Levi's Jeans because they were deemed cool. And I at least had to pretend to like the kind of music that was played on the local station, had to watch the popular movies and TV shows. And in order to do that, I had to accept—at least to some extent—the values the media promoted. To a large degree, I suppressed my individuality to fit in with the crowd in order to embrace values that weren't mine, that weren't really ours, but were values imposed upon us by commercial media. The values of my generation were the values of Coca Cola and record company executives. They were the values of sneaker manufacturers that exploited cheap labor abroad while giving millions of dollars to celebrity athletes to promote their brand. And I, either implicitly of complicitly, accepted such values.

Sometimes my friends and I talked about the superficiality of it all. Late at night. While drinking Mountain Dew and eating Doritos, when we were young. While drinking beer and smoking dope, when we were older. You see, back then, teenagers used to gather together and talk about things far away from the presence of the media. At a certain time of the night, the TV stations used to sign off the air, leaving nothing but a white noise which we had to fill with our own thoughts. We did not have unceasing access to the internet and the voices of advertisers, marketers and influencers people have today. The reach of the influencers was not so long. Places of sanctuary still existed, in schools, in churches, in the woods, or simply on a neighbor's front porch. On summer nights, it was not until our parents called us home that we were susceptible to the influence of the media.

Of course, then as now, the influence of the media never really left us. We carried it with us wherever we went. When we talked with each other, we talked about the movies we had watched, we stuck our thumbs up and said "Aaay!" the way The Fonz did. And when we discussed politics or social issues, we mostly echoed the opinions of those we got from the TV. Or that our parents got from TV.

I like to think I've reclaimed my independence from the social demands placed upon us by the media. It began, perhaps, when Levi's moved its manufacturing from union shops in the U.S. to sweat shops abroad, when I decided never again to buy the brand or associate myself with it. In a thousand ways since then, I have chosen not to buy what the media is selling us. But who is to say how much my decisions and attitude are still shaped by the media? On an almost daily basis, I notice some bias or belief drifting around in my mind that exists there only because the media told me something in my youth and I never stopped to question it. Like an adult who grew up in a dysfunctional family, there is much mental and spiritual work to be done.

There is this pseudo-reality constructed by the media that has been so pervasive we mistake it for the indisputable ultimate reality. While superficially it may appear that the power of the media has waned with the rise of social media and the internet, the truth is it has metastasized. The generation that raised mine—a generation all but gone now—was the last to be raised mostly free from the influence of the media. While the media is not as monolithic as it once was, its influence has not faded. It has become more creative, more devious, and more omnipresent. The matrix that was created by the television is now being strengthened by the same influencers with an even deeper and more persistent grasp on our psyches and nervous systems.

Philosophers and spiritual seekers in Ancient Greece, India and elsewhere have been able to perceive the illusions of the world and how much of what we believe to be is in fact not true. Perhaps in a sense our age is fortunate to have been presented with such a media matrix to serve as a model for the tricks our minds and egos play upon our consciousness. In any society, the dominant narratives will inevitably intertwine themselves with our own misunderstandings, will play upon our fears and insecurities.

Perhaps in exploring the ways in which the narratives of the media are mistaken for reality, we might better come to understand the ways in which other influences create illusions that we mistake to be truth. And perhaps in exploring the ways in which our minds can be fooled and unhealthy behavior patterns be allowed to develop, we can more clearly see just how much the narrative given to us by the media deviates from fact.

With that thought in my mind, I shall be releasing a companion book called Essays On Awakening, which should be available in early 2025. Feel free to follow me on Substack, Medium, Facebook, or Twitter to be updated on the release of this and other books to come. Thank you to all who have given me support, companionship, inspiration, and guidance. There are more of us than the media would like you to believe.

Thanks

Thanks to Dean Konop for the cover art.

Thanks to my wife Laura who has so much patience for such projects.

Thanks to Melissa Jindra, Joe Bakhos, Rista Croswell Prahar, Sam Rouse, Jill Klausen, Sara Behr, Cowt Owne and Melanie C. Norman for pre-purchasing my book, helping me to pay for the cover art.

Thanks to Melissa Jindra, Melanie C. Norman, Blake Rogers, and Laura Rozoff for your help in proofreading and your suggestions.

In memory of my brother Bob. You were my biggest supporter but you were also always there for me when I needed someone to point out spelling and grammatical errors. Though you are gone, you will forever remain on my list of people to thank.